THE FIVE THINGS
WE CANNOT CHANGE

THE
FIVE THINGS
WE CANNOT CHANGE

*And the Happiness
We Find by
Embracing Them*

DAVID RICHO

SHAMBHALA
Boston & London
2005

SHAMBHALA PUBLICATIONS, INC.
Horticultural Hall
300 Massachusetts Avenue
Boston, Massachusetts 02115
www.shambhala.com

9 8 7 6 5 4 3 2 1

First Edition
Printed in the United States of America

♾ This edition is printed on acid-free paper that meets
the American National Standards Institute z39.48 Standard.
Distributed in the United States by Random House, Inc.,
and in Canada by Random House of Canada Ltd

Library of Congress Cataloging-in-Publication Data
Richo, David, 1940–
The five things we cannot change: and the
happiness we find by embracing them / David Richo.—1st ed.
p. cm.
ISBN 1-59030-209-5 (pbk.: alk. paper)
1. Conduct of life. I. Title.
BF637.C5R535 2005
158—dc22
2004016055

*For my wonderfully
lovable nephews and niece,
Christian, Damien, and Thea*

*And in tender loving
memory of my sisters
Gail and Linda*

CONTENTS

PART TWO

AN UNCONDITIONAL YES
TO OUR CONDITIONED EXISTENCE

INTRODUCTION

THERE ARE some things in life over which we have no control, probably most things. We discover in the course of our lives that reality refuses to bow to our commands. Another force, sometimes with a sense of humor, usually comes into play with different plans. We are forced to let go when we want so much to hold on, and to hold on when we want so much to let go. Our lives—all our lives—include unexpected twists, unwanted endings, and challenges of every puzzling kind.

Reinhold Niebuhr, an American Protestant theologian, composed a prayer that has become the cornerstone of the recovery movement: "God grant me the serenity to accept the things I cannot change, the courage to change the things I can, and the wisdom to know the difference." This is a profound aspiration. But what are the things we cannot change? Are they unique to each of us, or are there some things that all of us must acknowledge and accept in order to find peace in our lives?

As a psychotherapist working with clients—and in my own life—I have seen the same questions and struggles arise again and again. There are five unavoidable givens, five immutable facts that come to visit all of us many times over:

1. Everything changes and ends.
2. Things do not always go according to plan.
3. Life is not always fair.
4. Pain is part of life.
5. People are not loving and loyal all the time.

These are the core challenges that we all face. But too often we live in denial of these facts. We behave as if somehow these givens aren't always in effect, or not applicable to all of us. But when we oppose these five basic truths we resist reality, and life then becomes an endless series of disappointments, frustrations, and sorrows.

In this book, I propose the somewhat radical idea that the five givens are not actually the bad news that they appear to be. In reality, our fear of and struggle against the givens are the real sources of our troubles. Once we learn to accept and embrace these fundamental, down-to-earth facts, we come to realize that they are exactly what we need to gain courage, compassion, and wisdom—in short, to find real happiness.

A given is a fact of life over which we are powerless. It is something we cannot change, something built into the very nature of things. From one point of view, there are many givens. In addition to the five disturbing givens stated above, there are also delightful givens: we experience bliss, our hopes are sometimes exceeded, we discover unique inner gifts, things have a way of working out, luck comes our way, miracles of healing happen.

There are also givens that apply only to us as individuals: our body shape and personality, our unique psychological and spiritual gifts or limitations, our temperament, our genetic makeup, our IQ, our conventional or unconventional lifestyle, whether we are introverted or extraverted, and so forth.

There are in fact, givens in every thing we do and in every place we enter. A given of having a job is that we might advance or we might be fired—as well as any number of possibilities between. A given of a relationship is that it may last a lifetime or it may end with the next phone call.

I have found that anything that crosses swords with our entitled ego is a powerful source of transformation and inner evolution. The five simple facts of life defy and terrorize the mighty ego that insists on full control. Life happens to us in its own way, no matter how much we may protest or seek to dodge it. No one is or has ever been exempt from life's uncompromising givens. If we cannot tolerate them, we add stress to our lives by fighting a losing game.

In this book I will explain why we need not feel despair in the face of the givens of our lives. We can learn to accept life on its own terms. We can even find its terms satisfactory. We do not have to shake our fist at heaven. We do not have to demand an exemption or take refuge in a belief system that muffles the wallop of the givens by promising a paradise without them. We can craft a sane and authentic life by saying yes to life just as it is. Indeed, our path is "what is."

The story of Buddha's enlightenment illustrates that the givens of life are the basis of our growth and transformation. The Buddha was born Siddhartha Gautama, an Indian prince. His father tried to protect him from encountering pain or displeasure. The king created a life of utter perfection for Siddhartha, providing him every possible satisfaction and shielding him from all unpleasantness. But one day the young prince wanted to see what lay beyond the palace walls. When he ventured out, he soon encountered sickness, old age, and death—the natural conditions of every life—for the first time. These sights moved him deeply and set him on a spiritual journey that ultimately led to his enlightenment. His legendary transformation began by facing the laws of life with curiosity and courage.

From ancient times, the five givens have puzzled and chagrined humanity. Religions offer responses to mysteries like these. Throughout this book I will draw on teachings from Buddhism and other world religions. Spiritual traditions offer us valuable resources, models, and inspiration for facing the givens of life openly and with equanimity. I rely most heavily on the Buddhist tradition because that spiritual tradition emphasizes the importance of seeing through our illusions and facing up to life's givens in order to become more fully who we are meant to be.

THE UNCONDITIONAL YES

Each of the givens or conditions of existence evokes a question about our destiny. Are we here to get our way or to dance with the flow of life? Are we here to make sure everything goes according to our plans or to trust the surprises and synchronicities that lead us to new vistas? Are we here to make sure we get a fair deal or are we here to be upright and loving? Are we here to avoid pain or to deal with it, grow from it, and learn to be compassionate through it? Are we here to be loyally loved by everyone or to love with all our might?

The ancient Romans spoke of *amor fati,* the virtue of loving one's fate. Some of us find it hard to handle the anxiety aroused by the conditions of our existence; we fight against our human situation. The method for handling the givens and gearing them to our destiny is stated most clearly by Carl Jung: "Givens can be embraced with an unconditional yes to that which is, without subjective protests, an acceptance of the conditions of existence . . . an acceptance of my own nature as I happen to be." Such a yes is a willingness to land on concrete reality without a pillow to buffer us. Such a yes makes us flexible, attuning us to a shifting world, opening us to whatever life brings. Such a yes is not a stoic surrender to the status quo but a courageous one—an alignment to reality. Once we trust reality more than our hopes and expectations, our yes becomes an "open sesame" to spiritual surprises. In this book, I will suggest how to discover the spiritual riches that lie within our most challenging experiences.

Yes is the brave ally of serenity; no is the scared accomplice of anxiety. We find help in saying yes and in facing the givens through mindfulness—that is, through fearless and patient attention of the present moment. We also gain support from nature, from psychology, from religious traditions, and from spiritual practices. These are the resources and tools presented in the pages that follow.

Hamlet speaks of "the thousand natural shocks that flesh is heir to," a poetic definition of the givens of life. When something happens to us that echoes with the painful thud of any of the unalterable conditions of existence, we can ask, "What can I learn here? How does

this serve?" We can learn to trust the givens of life as having trans-
formative or evolutionary potential. We can trust that the laws of existence somehow help us to achieve our destiny.

The givens of life may seem like cruel jokes perpetrated upon us
by a vindictive universe. They could seem like penalties for a way-
wardness we inherited but did not cause. They may even seem like
spiteful tricks to make our lives miserable. In an antiquated theological view, they are considered the punishments enacted by a vengeful
God upon us exiles from Eden for an original sin. The unconditional
yes, with its implicit trust of the givens' usefulness to our growth, cuts
through that fear-based view of life. Saying yes to reality—to the
things we cannot change—is like choosing to turn around and sit in
the saddle in the direction the horse is going. Sitting that way is mindfulness, an honoring of the here and now without the distractions of
fear or desire. Mindfulness is an unconditional yes to what is as it is.
We face our issues in the here and now without protest or blame.
Such a yes is unconditional because it is free of conditioning by the
neurotic ego: fear, desire, control, judgment, complaint, expectation.
When we are mindful, we meet each moment with openness, curiosity, and kindness. Mindfulness is both a state of being and a daily spiritual practice, a form of meditation.

WHY ME?

When faced with one of life's givens, we might ask: "Why did such a
terrible thing happen to a good person like me? I deserve better." The
mindful version of that question is: "Yes this happened. Now what?"
We will notice we are happier when we accept what we do not like
about life as a given *of* life. Our mindful yes is an entry into this sheltering paradox.

When we make an unreserved consent to the things we cannot
change, we are saying yes to ourselves, as we are, in our ever-
unfolding autobiography. The conditions of existence are our
personal experiences, not alien forces or hurdles to avoid. They are
also the universal experiences of all people. Every human who ever

lived faced the five major givens. This makes them part of being human, so they must be a *necessary* part. When we finally embrace the givens as extensions of our human selves, we say yes to them not in resignation or acquiescence. We say yes to the *ingredients* of our own humanity.

All the givens of life are based on one underlying fact: Anything can happen to anyone. This is the given of givens. Most of us have a hard time really believing this applies to us. We imagine that very good luck or very bad luck is supposed to happen to other people but never to us. To believe, finally and fully, that anything can happen to us is an enormously adult accomplishment, and it grants us two wonderful gifts. First, we let go of our ego's privileged view of itself as entitled to special treatment; we let go of the childlike belief that a rescuer, otherworldly or this-worldly, will come through just for us and grant us an exemption from life's hard knocks. Second, believing that anything can happen to us helps us become humble and helps us feel our comradeship with our fellow humans. "Nothing human is alien from me," the Roman poet Terence wrote in the second century B.C.E. There is something so consoling about a sense of belonging, of being in it with everyone else, no matter how difficult life may become.

The givens of life are a code to our personal evolution. An unconditional yes to the givens is how the code is broken or, rather, opened. In the traditional Buddhist view, birth as a human is a great boon. In the human realm there is said to be just the right mix of suffering and joy for us to awaken, to become enlightened. In other words, the givens of life help provide us with the perfect, awakening blend of experiences.

All things have a natural, irrepressible tendency to evolve, that is, to reach their full potential within the changing conditions of the environment. Therefore the hope we often feel so comforted by is not a foolish pipe dream. Hope is an authentic response to life's inherent, irrepressible inclination toward fulfillment. An unconditional—that is, mindful—yes to the givens, without debate or complaint, is all it takes.

GIVENS AS GIFTS

The word *given* has two meanings. It is a condition that cannot be changed, but it is also something that has been granted to us. Once we say yes, the givens of life are suddenly revealed as *gifts,* the skillful means to evolution. The givens are relentless but also rich with wisdom. Only amid such exacting and challenging conditions could we evolve. The givens of life are gifts because they are the ingredients of character, depth, and compassion.

What does it take to find the gift dimension in life's many challenges? First and foremost, we must cease our attempts to control or head them off. Then life's puzzling givens turn into doors to liberation. But we humans have a long tradition of reacting with defensiveness and resistance in the face of life's challenges. Indeed, our resistance to discomfort is part of our human inheritance. How ironic that we try so desperately to fend off what is unalterably our human condition and the conditions that can ultimately promote our growth.

The phrase "accepting the things we cannot change" makes it seem that we accept things only *because* we cannot change them. Actually, once we understand that what happens beyond our control may be just what we need, we see that acceptance of reality can be our way of participating in our own evolution. Serenity comes not only from accepting what we cannot change but from giving up trying to be in control. There is meaning in events that happen and this meaning is multileveled, so we will address this subject often throughout the book.

The unconditional yes makes us ready for joy or pain. Accepting the world on its terms is living a heroic life. In the classical hero myths there is always a struggle phase when the hero must confront the conditions of existence. A hero is someone who has lived through pain, been transformed by it, and uses it to help others. As Shakespeare says in *King Lear:*

A most poor man, made tame to fortune's
    blows,
Who by the art of known and feeling sorrows
Am pregnant to good pity.

The givens of his life *equip* Lear to have compassion toward others. Our spiritual work is not merely personal. We individuals are continually being ignited with a fiery urge to activate the evolutionary possibilities of the collective human spirit. Ultimately, we engage in spiritual practice so we can bring all humanity along with us to enlightenment. Indeed, it is a built-in feature of goodness to give of itself: as Aristotle says, "Goodness cannot help but diffuse itself."

Beings as complex and creative as we are could not be satisfied in a world without soul-stretching givens. Shakespeare, Mozart, and Einstein would not have appeared in a world in which things did not change and end, things were fully predictable, life did not include pain, and everyone loyally loved us. That world would be superficial and ultimately "dull, flat, stale, and unprofitable," as Hamlet says of his limited world.

Creative people appreciate the conditions of existence as having meaning beyond the meanings society may impose. They refashion the givens of life as works of art. This is because the givens are wellsprings of creativity and of new possibilities. Our own and the world's imperfections become the raw material for a masterpiece. The artist takes it in and digests it into something useful to and edifying for others, like a bird that feeds its young with food it has swallowed.

GIVENS AS GRACES

To find real happiness in life takes developing ourselves emotionally and spiritually. Spiritual consciousness breaks through dualism, through our simplistic notions of good and bad. An unconditional yes is a yes to the paradoxes of life. A paradox combines apparent opposites. For instance, we say yes unconditionally to an existence conditioned by changes and endings. We can make commitments even though plans fall through. We can maintain our compassion no matter how unjust the world may be to us. We can be loving toward others no matter how cruelly they act toward us. Nothing that happens to us has to dismount us from the horse called Yes. We can recognize people's dark side and yet we do not give up on them, another feature of spiritual maturity.

Here are other examples of the paradoxes we can joyously embrace as we recognize the value of the givens:

Although *everything changes and ends,* things renew themselves and move through cycles that further evolution.

Although *things do not always go according to plan,* we sometimes sense a larger plan at work through synchronicity that opens startling possibilities.

Although *life is not always fair,* something in us remains committed to fairness and refuses to be unjust or retaliatory.

Although *suffering is part of life,* we have ways of dealing with it and thereby we expand our powers to handle future pain and help others in their pain.

Although *people are not loving and loyal all the time,* nothing has to get in the way of our acting with loving-kindness and not giving up on others. No human action can take away another human being's capacity to love.

The givens are stated in ways that may seem negative but each has a positive side. The paradoxes above show the positive dimension in each of the conditions of existence. Every time a given is answered with a yes, we develop emotionally and spiritually: we advance in patience, forbearance, forgiveness, generosity, wisdom, appreciation, perseverance, and unconditional love.

Yet ultimately, the fact that there is much in life that we cannot control means that we may need a special boost, something our ego cannot provide, something our limited mind cannot conceive, something our frail will cannot effect. This is the assisting force of *grace,* the spiritual complement to effort. Something kicks in that is bigger than us and makes our path easier to tread.

The Upanishads, sacred texts of Hinduism, refer to grace this way: "The Self [truth] cannot be gained by the Vedas [scriptures], nor by understanding, nor by learning. He whom the Self chooses, by him the Self is gained." Grace is a gift of the higher Self to the ego. A source beyond ego grants us the gift of transcending our ordinary limits. Grace means that we are not alone; we are always accompanied:

When we are sure we can't get through another minute and we do, that is the grace of a Creator life in us.
When we are sure we can't find the light and we do, that is the grace of the Light of the World in us.
When we are sure we can't take one more breath and we do, that is the grace of the Spirit breathing through us.

Our hearts were hewn by light. The unconditional yes helps our heart let its light through. Graces are those special gifts that break through our limits of mind, will, and heart. Grace expands our intellect by endowing us with intuitive wisdom. We suddenly become inspired by something we did not find through logic. Grace expands our will by giving us a strength or courage we did not have before. Grace expands our hearts by making it possible to love rather than hate, to reconcile rather than retaliate, to show humility rather than hubris. We could not do all that on our own; our self-centered ego would find no motivation for such virtue. Grace is the inner ally and guide, the motivating force of our spiritual practice.

As givens become graces, an unconditional thanks stands beside our unconditional yes. When we accept the good with the bad, the easy with the difficult, gratitude arises automatically. Hamlet said to Horatio:

Thou hast been as one . . . that fortune's
    buffets and rewards
Hast taken with equal thanks.

Each given of life comes to us trailing many graces. The fact that things change and end means that we may find in impermanence the grace of flowing with life. Health, both psychologically and spiritually, means going with the flow of events, rather than being stopped or devastated by them. The fact that things do not always go according to plan means that many powers beyond ego are at work in our lives—powers that lead us to our destiny by a path we might have neglected. Once we understand that we are supported by powers beyond our ego, we see that having to be in control may not be in our best interest: we might upset mighty plans that are afoot on our behalf.

The fact that life is not always fair even though we know instinctively what would be fair means that we are all called to create the conditions of justice in the world. When we say yes to such a call, we find our courage. Then we find ways of balancing ourselves and assisting the world in balancing itself.

The fact that pain is part of life yields the graces of endurance, patience, and compassion. We are affected by others' pain and less likely to be sources of pain to others.

The fact that others are not always loyal or loving inflicts the wounds that make us people of depth and character. Perhaps such wounds are graces since the holes in us can be openings to wholeness. And, most of all, we are thereby challenged to show an unconditional love.

Grace is not soporific; it arrives bugle-in-hand. Each grace is a reveille to rouse our effort. In this book I hope to show how graces are offered to us in the form of the givens. In addition, if we have the courage to face life's unavoidable truths, we will find the grace to love no matter what happens to us. Love is always unconditional in the sense that it is not stymied or stifled by any of the conditions of existence. Neither changes, endings, altered plans, unfairness, suffering, disloyalty, or lack of love can stop us from loving. Our yes to such a stunning grace is what our ego always wants to say, since it means the end of being afraid and the beginning of being free.

PART ONE
THE GIVENS OF LIFE

Facing the bluntness of reality is the highest form of sanity and enlightened vision. . . . Devotion proceeds through various stages of unmasking until we reach the point of seeing the world directly and simply without imposing our fabrications. . . . There may be a sense of being lost or exposed, a sense of vulnerability. That is simply a sign that ego is losing its grip on its territory; it is not a threat.

—Chögyam Trungpa Rinpoche

ONE

EVERYTHING CHANGES
AND ENDS

THE FIRST GIVEN of life is that changes and endings are inevitable for any person, relationship, enthusiasm, or thing. Nothing is perfect, permanently satisfying, or permanently anything. Everything falls apart in time. Every beginning leads to a finale. Built into all experiences, persons, places, and things is a life span. Our relationships pass through phases, from romance through struggle to commitment. Then they end with death or separation. Our interest in hobbies or careers passes over a bell-shaped curve of rising interest, cresting, and decline. Our bodies age. Our possessions deteriorate. Our memories wane. The world of nature changes too. Species of animals disappear. Earthquakes realign the continental plates. Seasons change. Even the rose will fade after her stunning debut.

Yet once we trust the process of evolution, we realize that the way things are must be exactly what is best. The changes are carefully timed alignments that make the universe endure and unfold. This is ultimately a mystery, since it is hard to know why it has to be this way. All we can observe is that life is committed to variety and new growth, and that comes at the price of endings. Perhaps things end so that we can reach the high spiritual peak that comes with letting go. This too is a mystery, and in the face of it, the only sensible etiquette is to change our "Why?" to "Yes."

We can welcome life's givens. The unconditional yes is hospitality to life in any guise in which it visits us. In the book of Genesis, Sara and Abraham gave hospitality to three strangers, unaware that they were angels. In Greek mythology, Philemon and Baucis were hospitable to two passersby, Zeus and Hermes in disguise. Thus hospitality can reveal the divine in the unknown. A welcoming yes reveals and alerts us to the spiritual world. To say yes to reality is to host eternity. To say yes to the finite and limited is to host the infinite and the limitless.

The fact that reality is impermanent does not have to mean that it is trivial, useless, or superficial. It can be an indication of the holiness of things. Holiness is wholeness. The sense of the holy is consciousness of the sacred possibilities in finite events. Holiness is the *whole* condition of things, events, and human relationships: beginnings and endings too.

Does impermanence have to cancel our chances at happiness? Ecclesiastes 1:2 warns: "Vanity of vanities; all is vanity." The Hebrew word translated as *vanity* more literally means "thin air." Yet in that same book we are told to enjoy life with our partner, to eat and drink wine with a merry heart, and to do our daily work with exuberance (Eccles. 9:7–10). The answer to the unappealing way of all flesh is to enjoy fleshly things nonetheless. A path into the mystery of change and ending may be that of paradox: saying yes with gusto to what is unsatisfactory.

HOW WE AVOID OR ACCEPT

Meister Eckhart wrote: "Everything is meant to be let go of that the soul may stand in unhampered nothingness." Imagine the depth of spiritual consciousness in that statement. It can be ours as well as his. First we look at everything about us and around us and say: All this will go. Then we contemplate ourselves without all we cling to and say: "I want to be unencumbered. I want to be purely no-thing. I want to stand in the full monty of yes."

In our culture we continually avoid looking at the reality of change and death. We act as if we were unable to handle them. Yet we come equipped with an organic, reliable, inner technology for dealing with losses and endings: We can mourn. Unless we override or numb our feelings, we can automatically feel sad, angry, and afraid when loss occurs. These are the feelings of grief that help us work through the unappealing facts of death and endings. Mourning is what yes looks like when we face the conditions of existence with feeling. The fact that we are able to grieve tells us we were meant to face losses and endings and to resolve them. Our very nature, like nature itself, is calibrated to deal with death rather than to deny it. Indeed, death will not be foreign to those who have spent their adult lives letting go of ego and its adhesions. Grief, the yes of tears, makes possible an acceptance of reality and its conditions, including an ending in death. Since every one of the givens of life represents a loss, grief work is a skillful means with which to face them all. As long as we buy into society's denial of the need for grief, we lose our chance at strength in the face of what life brings. It is up to us to allow the mourning that all life's conditions require. It is up to us to trust that mourning is precisely how we resolve our losses and move through them to what comes next, the evolutionary style.

To go through the experience of mourning a partner or family member, for instance, leads to letting go of whomever we lost. Grief readies us eventually to give up clinging to the past and to move toward closeness with new others who offer approximations of what we lost. We will not recover a mother, but we can experience motherly moments with nurturant others. Thus we feel no longer alone and isolated but reconciled to reality and reconnected to other humans. In fact, reconciliation is the ability to accept an approximation. This is the yes of healthy compromise.

ATTRACTED OR REPELLED

Our attractions and repulsions to people, places, and things seem to flow over a bell-shaped curve. We notice three phases in the curve: rising, cresting, falling. We hear a song and get to love it (rising interest), so we buy the CD and listen to it constantly (cresting enjoyment). Then we listen less frequently (falling off of interest), and finally, what was the best song we ever heard is rarely listened to again. Its appeal went over the hill of the bell curve.

This same bell curve happens with repulsions, as the story of Beauty and the Beast depicts. At first Beauty felt disgust, but later she felt love. Since it is a fairy tale, the positive high crest remains: "happily ever after." Demanding that the high crest of any experience be permanent is living in a fairy tale.

Another example of the curve in repulsion is found in how we react to a monster in a horror film. At first sight we turn away in fear or disgust. But as the monster continues to appear in scene after scene, we grow accustomed to the monster's face and are no longer scared. Indeed, the bell-shaped curve, an inner geometric figure in all of us, is what makes for fearlessness.

Intimate relationships follow this same pattern. "It's not the way it used to be," we say of a relationship. We grow in romantic feelings, get to a crest of excitement, and then notice that the thrill is gone. Our choices are two. We can break up or we can fashion a new, more mature love based not on thrill but on commitment. The biggest mistake we humans make is to become attached to someone's being a certain way and then to think that will never change. Recalling the story by Goethe, Faust made a pact with the devil. He would lose his soul if ever he said: "Abide, thou art so fair." We lose our spiritual life when we try to hold on to perfection or changelessness.

In the ongoing project of denying the conditions of existence, we may recruit a partner. Intimate relationships become more crucial to survival in a society in which religion wanes in meaning. Relationships become the new refuge, the new higher power. The collective has yielded to the personal. With no Spirit above, we grasp more tightly the body below. So the failure of a relationship conveys a double grief, even panic.

Each of the five main givens of life confront our deeply held illusions. The fact that things change confronts the illusion of permanence. The fact that plans fall through confronts our illusion of control. Our illusion that things will be fair or that pain will not happen to us or that people will be trustworthy are all called into question by the givens we face in the course of life. The givens liberate us from ignorance and illusion.

In a practice such as mindfulness, we cultivate attention to the here and now without our interfering story lines or editing. This is how we are liberated from illusion. Mindfulness escorts us to the middle path between attraction and repulsion. We do not become attached to what is appealing nor do we flee what is repulsive. We simply sit in our present reality and notice our desires to draw near or withdraw without having to act on them. In this center position is the yes to the total reality rather than the no to one or another dimension of it. This choice is for psychological work *and* spiritual practice.

Psychologically, it makes sense to move toward or away from things. It is a sign of healthy discretion, discernment, and assertiveness. Psychology is the science of the ego, and the ego thrives on distinctions and choices. Yet "either . . . or" does not make room for the spiritual dimension of discernment. It is ignorance, the insistence on one option instead of an embrace of all the possibilities within the spectrum.

Spiritual flexibility thrives on the reconciliation of apparent contradictions. It is the science of paradox, that is, "both . . . and." For instance, in Buddhist practice the bodhisattva vows enjoin the practitioner to put others first. This same commitment is in "Love thy neighbor," a feature of all religious traditions. Yet assertiveness—a psychological skill—is about putting ourselves first without harming others. How do we reconcile these two recommendations?

The answer is in distinguishing the provinces of each dimension of life. In psychological work, we work with duality, since our "self" is in our uniqueness. In spiritual practice we encounter no dualism at all, since we have no "either . . . or" self, only a "both . . . and" interconnectedness. I take care of myself but not at the expense of others; I put others first but not at the expense of myself.

In the self-help movement, we learn about integrating our psychological work and our spiritual practice, but we may not notice an important distinction: They are not the same, since one is dualistic and one is not. The integration is the task of paradox whereby we acknowledge the differences and find a way to live *between* them. In that middle path is the balance that puts the word *unconditional* into the unconditional yes, that is, no longer conditioned or determined by an "either . . . or."

"Both . . . and" reflects the teachings of the Buddhist tantric tradition, in which the conditions of existence are embraced as the useful raw material of spiritual practice. Our personal problems and interpersonal conflicts become the path to compassion and wisdom. We neither deny nor avoid the feelings that life's conditions arouse. The givens and our responses are essential ingredients for enlightenment. This makes the world itself an epiphany of light. Tantra makes our evolution of consciousness a primal and indestructible unity. Indeed, consciousness *is* the life force of the universe.

We continue to notice in these pages how every vehicle of yes—spiritual, mystical, psychological—to the givens of life endorses and prizes our interconnectedness. This is a planetization of consciousness. It is not only our personal consciousness that is increasing but also our collective capacity for consciousness. Our personal light increases the world's capacity for light.

GROWING OLDER: A CHANGING IMAGE IN THE MIRROR

Our personality also passes through phases throughout our life span. Our at times arrogant ego of adolescence grows in ambition and the sense of invincibility through early adulthood. We are making our mark in the world and pushing everything aside to get to the top. We are able to push our bodies with no negative health effects. As we pass forty-five, things change. If we say yes to the change, we move through it with grace and aplomb. If we fight it or try to extend the youthful style, we find ourselves in a midlife crisis or with health problems.

The psychological challenge is to accept the given that our ego was only temporarily in charge and was eventually meant to reconcile itself to a humbler station. This does not mean we are useless or moribund, only that we are now in a new phase of life, one that may have less glamour but more wisdom. Our life moves from the surf at Waikiki to Golden Pond.

When my eyes began to focus less accurately in reading, I at first denied that any loss was happening in my vision. Then I started using a magnifying glass. Soon I switched to the store-bought magnifying eyeglasses, still refusing to visit the eye doctor. As headaches began, I finally went to the optometrist, who gave me a prescription. I recall his having to assure me I was getting the weakest lenses, not anything that represented true need. I could tell he had met my type before: an aging guy trying to deny it is time to let go. My body said yes long before my mind could follow suit.

Our bodies help us say yes because they alter in shape, prowess, and powers all through life. Our bodies resolutely declare the noble truth of impermanence. In a way, all the givens are noble truths: They tell the universal story of a human life span and invite us to follow it rather than attempt to revise it in accord with the wishes of our ever-unsatisfied ego. As we age, we can gracefully accede to the withering alterations. Such a yes frees us from being overly concerned about appearance. Nature can then relocate our focus on wisdom, something that aging makes us ready to find and share. The more superficial our focus remains, the less likely is this to happen. Then we miss out on fulfilling the archetype of the wise guide for the generation that follows us.

Why are people of all ages on the planet at once? Each has a necessary role, one that changes throughout life. I am the young Turk and then the old sage. If my focus is on the material, I am the old miser and miss my chance to contribute. If my focus is on the physical, I am the old narcissist and miss my chance to be generous. This does not mean that it is wrong to want to look one's best. The danger is in becoming so obsessed with our appearance that our vanity deafens us to our destiny.

Our society is youth obsessed, and without a spiritually mature consciousness we can fall prey to its seductive suggestions. How sad it would be to come to the end of our life without having let our natural inclination toward wisdom be activated as fully as it can be. A yes to the fact that all things change and end is a yes to letting nature have its way with us. This often means wrinkles *and* wisdom. Somehow they usually go together, although wisdom can come as a grace at any age, and yes, wrinkles can appear with little wisdom in their wake. We cannot control the process or be guaranteed the wisdom, but an unconditional yes places us in the best position to let the light through.

WHAT MAKES US SO CONTROLLING

The opposite of yes is not no; it is control. Behind that controlling impulse is fear, the fear that we will have to feel something painful. Every given insults the ego that wants to believe it has full control. Yes is acceptance; control is refusal. We can learn to accept the fact that we are sometimes helpless to stop an unwelcome change in our lives. That acceptance, paradoxically, ushers in serenity. Trying to stay fully in control of what will happen to us makes us opponents of life's facts and maintains stress. Our life is a seesaw tottering between terror and control as long as we stutter at the word *yes*.

To let go of control will mean that we cannot protect ourselves from any of the givens. Control is one of our favorite ways of running from life as it is. Control is so deeply engrained an illusion that we even think we can let go of control simply by wanting to. We do not let go of control; we let go of the belief that we have control. The rest is grace. The givens of life are the tools the universe provides for that lesson.

Worry is directly related to control. It seems that we worry about the future, finances, relationships, jobs, and all the other unpredictables in our lives. Actually, there is only one worry: that of not being in full control of what will happen. We worry because we do not trust ourselves to handle what happens to us. We worry because we do not trust that the way the chips fall will work out for the best. We worry because we have not yet said yes. *I am noticing that now that I am practicing the unconditional yes, I worry less.*

When we begin to say yes to the realities of our lives, it's important to remember not to push our particular yes onto others, since we all have a different reality to affirm. As I was altering my diet to healthy foods, I recall reminding my then twenty-year-old son, Josh, to stay away from junk food. His answer remains in my mind: "There is plenty of time for me. I can eat junk food with no negative effects. When the time comes to switch to health food, I will know and make the change then." Not totally true but in the ballpark. I was imposing my new yes on his young body, and he would not buy it.

I am now more careful with Josh and with everyone not to become the CIA: Critic, Interpreter, and Advisor. We can make it a spiritual practice not to criticize others' behavior, not to interpret what they do according to our worldview, and not to advise unless we are invited to do so. Eliminating these three behaviors from our repertory, especially with partners and family members, makes our communication much more loving and respectful. The five essential qualities of genuine love—attention, acceptance, appreciation, affection, and allowing (what I call the five A's)—do not survive well with the CIA in pursuit.

Why is control such a big deal for most of us? Perhaps we are trying to head off losses by controlling. We will not have to mourn if everything comes out our way. We do not control because we are selfish or demanding. We control because we are afraid of grief. It is no fun having to feel sad. It hurts to let ourselves know how and what we lost. Our threadbare ego is insulted and feels impotent, and that is intolerable to us. As long as we can stay in control, we will avoid all those invitations to humility. This is a compassionate take on why we are so damn controlling.

Our spiritual work is to live more fully in the present. The first given of life, the fact of impermanence, means that everything in our lives will keep changing. Joseph Campbell says: "Hell is being stuck in ego," stuck in trying to control things so that they stay the same. By practice and grace, we can awaken into a new consciousness. The ever-present and ineradicable opportunity to change is a reason never to give up on ourselves or others. Then even hell is impermanent.

When we give up what in *Hamlet* is called "our peevish opposition" to life's givens, we throw in our lot with that of the rest of humanity. Then we are not alone and our negotiations with the world no longer break down. They hook up felicitously and so do we. We hold our heads heavenward when we ride in the direction in which reality is going. This means living life with no trimmings, no frills, no buffers, no godfather to cover for us. Instead, we love to uncover our bare hearts and discard our tinsel armor: I am no longer so concerned with being in control of what I am like. I am becoming curious about what I will be like.

As long as we are feuding with life's rules, we will fear the direct contact with reality that is the essence of true growth. We will find mindfulness difficult because it insists on full presence in the moment as it is. We may enlist many outs to protect ourselves: money, sex, alcohol, coffee, food, smoking, drugs, and, of course, the ceaseless movements of our frantic mind itself with all its hopes and fears. When we look deeply into our fears, we see that, at base, every fear is a fear of not having control.

We may not notice the control issue in some of the experiences that bother us on a daily basis. Control remains the opponent of a healthy and robust yes to reality as it is. It is not that we resent reality; we resent not being in control of it. If we look closely, we might see a control dimension in annoyances like these:

We want to be different from the way we are.
We want others to be different.
We want someone to call back or visit.
We do not like tests or waiting for results.
The house is not as clean and neat as we want it to be.
We cannot get rid of the ants or roaches once and for all.
We cannot keep the weight off or the blood pressure down.
We obsess about what happened or what might happen.
We have feelings, moods, and habits that we do not like.
We do not sleep as well as we want to.
Our parents, children, partners, or friends do not act as we want them to.
We feel compelled to anticipate all possibilities.
We cannot get certain people to like us no matter how hard we try.

We were not successful at a job, in a relationship, or in financial
    planning.
We thought of what to say only after an altercation.
We lack skill in mathematics, baseball, or gardening.

Underlying every one of these is the belief that we should be in
control of everything at all times. That ironic enslavement makes for
anxiety. It is the opposite of the serenity promised by its alternative,
an unconditional yes to what is and to ourselves and others as we happen to be.

How does needing to be in control help or hinder us in facing the
givens of life, the living conditions here on earth? In a world in which
things change and end, an attitude of acceptance and trust makes
sense. This is impossible without letting go of control. In a world in
which control is not reliable, we need something else: the ability to be
satisfied with doing our best and letting the chips fall where they may.
Then the work is to deal with what happens, however unkempt or in-
decipherable it may be. To focus on being in control hinders our
chances of finding the new possibilities that arise when surprising directions appear on our path. Randomness becomes less scary and
more appealing when we find in it a new frontier.

An example of how life and destiny happen in surprising ways is
apparent in the life of author Margaret Mitchell. She worked as a
journalist in her native Atlanta with no evident interest in writing fic-
tion. One day she was thrown from her horse and was forced to stay
at home for months of recuperation. To pass the time, she began writing a romantic novel about Atlanta in Civil War times. She worked
on it for ten years. *Gone with the Wind,* published in 1936, won the
Pulitzer Prize and became her legacy to the world.

NOTHING SEPARATE

Aldous Huxley commented that the phrase "I am" has two errors in
it: *I* gives the impression of separateness; *am* gives the impression of
permanence. Yet it seems to be a given of ecology that there is no

separateness and a given of physical existence that everything is changing. These two concepts are connected, since, when all is inter-related—no separate I—we are not at odds with the given of impermanence. When we feel desperate to create some secure moorings, we are fleeing the spirit-building given of life that everything is meant to change and shift.

The Buddhist practice of mindfulness acknowledges the suffering that characterizes change and impermanence and recommends not an escape from suffering but an attention to it. We sit through what happens without the interferences of ego—fear, desire, control, judgment, illusion, complaint. We contribute to our own suffering when we engage in ego fear and desire rather than simply being here now as breathing beings who are continually in the midst of current events. As we pare down our predicament to just what it is, without editorial comment, and say yes to it, we cease battling reality. To say yes is to access another voice in us besides that of our ventriloquist plaintiff ego. Yes reflects our true nature—our buddha nature—back to us, the fair and alert witness within.

Reality does not accede to our wishes or plans but remains intent upon its own narrow path. To stand in opposition to reality is certainly a cause of suffering. To be free of the influence of an interfering ego therefore implies freedom from suffering. We let go of a belief in permanence because the clinging that results is a cause of suffering. The ego loves to grab and cling but finds only disquietude and disappointment that way. We let go so we can be happy. Letting go is not a loss but an emancipation.

We are faced with two axes on which to live. Each axis centers around hope:

We can live by faith, hope, and love, the axis of light. We can live by fear, hope, and greed, the axis of darkness. In addition, looking at the vertical column on the right, we see that true love cancels fear. On the left side, faith makes clinging or greed unnecessary, since we sparrows can trust that we will have what we need without a barn overfull of grain. Horizontally, love, with its wonderful capacity for trust and letting go, frees us from greed. Faith frees us from fear, because it too is trust. Hope, which can be either positive or negative, is the hub of all our inclinations. Negatively, it can keep us stuck or attached. Positively it is the trust that darkness is not permanent but rather an eclipse after which the light will return. Hope is the unconditional gift to us curious craving Pandoras who move from one axis to another so many times in the course of life.

A TWO-HANDED PRACTICE

I am aware that I will always be fearful in some way. But I do not have to be fear-based in my behavior or choices. I can hold my fear in one hand and my commitment to no longer act in a fear-based way in the other. Somehow that combination seems more doable than no fear at all.

A useful spiritual practice in any predicament is to hold both hands out, cupped, palms upward, and imagine them holding just such opposites. We feel the light and equal weight of both, since our hands are empty. We then say, for example, "I can serenely hold both my need for relationship and my not having one right now."

Here is another example: I lose my job and am depressed and scared. At the same time, I know I have to search for another job. I hold my unemployed situation in one hand with serene acceptance of the reality of my loss. I hold my plan to do a job search in the other. This is how my depression, a given of every life from time to time, does not descend into despair. Holding my opposites grants me serenity and courage. This practice combines the style of mindfulness with psychological work on self-esteem.

I can sit in my predicament as a witness, not as a plaintiff or judge: "Here I am in this situation and I sit squarely in it and breathe into it. At the same time, I am aware that I can handle this and get through it without becoming devastated. I can trust my competence neither to become dramatically overwhelmed nor to be stoically untouched. This sense of competence frees me from fear, since fear thrives on powerlessness. I imagine myself holding my predicament in one hand and my power to work with it in the other. One hand is serenely mindful; one is courageously working. When I hold both realities this way, I am agreeable to things as they are, and I am doing all I can to change them for the better as well. As I grow in the courage to change what can be changed and the serenity to accept what cannot be changed, I find the wisdom to know the difference. As of now, I affirm that I am able to handle whatever may happen for the rest of my life. I have handled so much so far, I know I will be able to face whatever is left. And if I need reinforcements, I will find them. Nothing will turn my life so upside down that I will collapse under it."

Our limits on self-acceptance are equal to the limits on our power to activate ourselves. The more we believe in our competence to reconstitute our broken state, the less we feel the fear that keeps us that way. Any event held in both hands combines reality with hope for renewal. That is what handling something means.

DEATH AND RENEWAL

The prominence of sacrifice in the course of history shows that the ache of loss and change can be meaningful. An evolutionary opportunity awaits us when we follow the model of nature. Everything in nature is going through what we have to go through, and it is showing us how.

In Japanese Zen, nature is certainly understood as integral to enlightenment. Natural things are not separate but interconnected in Buddha's ecological view. Hakuin, an eighteenth-century Japanese Zen master, says: "From the beginning there is not a single [separate] thing." The truth of impermanence is visible in nature, since things keep changing. The truth of the importance of nonattachment comes through as we notice that things exist only as they are, not necessarily as we want them to be. This is not only Buddha's truth. It appears in many traditions. Catholic mystic Hildegard of Bingen says: "Everything that is in the heavens, on the earth, and under the earth is penetrated with connectedness, penetrated with relatedness."

Most of us fear the thought of death, and we surround ourselves with things and people who may perpetuate the illusion of permanence. We fear loss, so we gather and grasp. To face the reality of endings, our own and others', is yet another way to foster spiritual vision. Our ending is a return to the Source: human nature folding back into its origins. What we imagine to be merely mortal turns out to have "immortal longings" built into it—as Shakespeare's Cleopatra says.

Nature deals with death by renewal in cycles and in procreation. Awareness of our own creatureliness helps us join in more willingly. To say yes to life and death is to transcend them. Immortality may be a way of describing this non-time-bound dimension of our being, what Jung called the Self. This can happen when we transition from egocentric living to cosmo-centric living—our larger life in loving-kindness. Indeed, immortality may be what happens when we join the process of evolution and make its goals our own. If biological evolution were only about survival, rats would have been as far as nature needed to go. We are here because evolution is about love.

Early peoples, in their burial rituals, displayed an intuitive consciousness of renewal and return. This is the collective archetype of resurrection that has fascinated humanity from the beginning. Nature figures prominently in rituals of resurrection. For example, at a Lebanon burial site, the dead person was buried with a deer to provide food in the afterlife. In addition, an artistic layout of painted stones was placed around the corpse. In other early burial sites, pollens of hyacinths found among bones indicated that flowers were placed on bodies in prehistoric burial rites. The hyacinth, returning every spring, is in fact a universal symbol of resurrection. The things in nature are thus accommodations that nature makes with humans to stamp their passport to the archetypal world.

Nature has always been honored as having sacramental power. A sacrament is a ritual that effects spiritually what it displays materially, for example, baptism "washes away" sin. All sacraments use the things of nature to evoke spiritual power. Every religious tradition includes rituals and sacraments that honor nature as having powers to effect transitions. This is acknowledging the spiritual dimension of nature. Anything that says nothing but yes is certainly spiritual. The givens become sacraments—sources of grace—when we say yes too.

Is our belief in an afterlife or rebirth a fact of the archetypal world or a buffer against the thud of the first given of life, which is that life ends? Eternal life may not be the same as an afterlife. It may mean a larger life than ego can ever comprehend. It may mean entering interconnectedness and finally being liberated from the illusion of separateness. It may mean continuing to return through rebirths. We recall Einstein's statement that energy can neither be created nor destroyed.

Perhaps we do not need evidence of eternal life or even to know what it is like. Perhaps we need only a faith in the force of surrender to the givens of human existence. The surrender is to become part of something greater than our ego, that is, our interconnectedness beyond ego. Surrender is not despairing of ourselves or becoming self-abnegating in any way. In spiritual consciousness we never give up on anyone, not even ourselves.

An unconditional yes has power over life and death. That is the faith that becomes stronger, paradoxically, as we accept death and leave the rest to this vast universe from which we somehow have come and to which we somehow return. Our reabsorption in the vastness of being may be an equivalent of eternal life. The Milky Way then becomes simultaneously spouse, child, and mother.

We do not know how we live on or how the promise of immortality can be kept. But perhaps if we assent more amiably to the inexorable fact that we will die, we may find in that very surrender a glimpse into another way of living, one that exults valiantly in a yes both to what is and to whatever will be. That can feel like immortality. Death may be a handing over of the ego's kingdom—and the body, its palace—to the league of stars and seas. The mystical body of the universe reabsorbs our energy and redistributes it in accord with whatever level of evolution we achieved during our brief, uneasy, and ecstatic reign.

All we have to trust is the paradox of nature: to let go every instant and yet be entirely here and now. Then, as we find in the poem "What Are Years?" by Marianne Moore: "He . . . is glad who accedes to mortality . . . as the sea . . . in its surrendering find, its continuing."

As I say yes to the givens of life, may I welcome the springs and winters of my life with equal thanks, and may I always be able to guide and calm those who cling to life too tightly or run from death too frantically.

TWO

THINGS DO NOT ALWAYS GO ACCORDING TO PLAN

For all that has been: Thanks!
For all that shall be: Yes!
　　　　　　　—DAG HAMMARSKJÖLD, *Markings*

Ｉｎ ｔｈｅ ｅａｒｌｙ 1940s, on the night of her graduation party, a high school girl named Doris Van Kappelhoff was involved in a serious car accident. She had planned to go to Hollywood to become a dancer in films, but her injuries made that future no longer possible. Doris, during her long homebound recuperation, began to sing along with the female vocalists on the radio. Her voice became so well trained that she was hired to sing in a band, and soon thereafter, she found parts in movies, changing her name to Doris Day. Her original plans were dashed by a tragic event, but thereby she found her true calling. Things don't always go according to our plans, but a change of plans may be an example of synchronicity, the mysterious set of coincidental circumstances that lead us to a life fulfillment unguessed and unsought—other words for grace.

We make plans expecting to be in control of what will happen.

Perhaps we fear natural happenings, things turning out contrary to our wishes. We are challenged by life's "mind of its own" to let go of having things come out our way. This is about control. We may act with precision, and self-discipline, expecting the world to follow suit and grant us our reward.

Perfect discipline, or perfect control, is the best way to miss out on the joy of life. The unruly givens of life are permissions not to be perfect. We can flow into the natural chaos of life, so untidy, so unpredictable, or we can try to order life fully by making careful plans. But as Robert Burns says to a mouse: "The best-laid schemes of mice and men oft go astray and leave us naught but grief and pain for promised joy." We know now that a yes to life is a yes to grief and pain, since all the conditions of existence represent losses and disappointments. Yes is a healthy response to the human condition.

Making plans is an adult occupation, a feature of the healthy ego. In fact, though, life often does not proceed according to our plans. This does not have to leave us crestfallen. It can make us excited that something spiritual, that is, unconjured by ego, may be afoot. Perhaps we believe the universe has a plan that more accurately reflects our emerging destiny. Perhaps we believe there is no plan at all and "them's the breaks." As adults we do not console ourselves with promises of a silver lining in every cloud or a Shangri-la in any land. Our comfort is in our commitment to deal with what happens and make the best of it. Or are we angry that the givens make us keep having to grow up?

To grow into adulthood means that we accept the givens of life as they are, and this helps us accept ourselves as we are. Being an adult means living with life's conditions in an allowing way.

Maybe we don't fit psychology's definition of "well-adjusted," or maybe we didn't benefit from healthy emotional development. We did not have a perfect childhood or a perfect adolescence, and we are not having a perfect adulthood. All our investments are not paying off. All our hopes for the future are not coming true. Life is unpredictable and not at our beck and call. Can that become palatable? Can that be appreciated as somehow useful to our becoming people of character, depth, and compassion? Then to complain is to have missed the point.

In a world in which I may not do or finish anything perfectly or get anything permanently right, it makes sense to let go of the need for perfection. The Bhagavad Gita says: "Even a little progress is complete freedom from fear." Can I be satisfied with that as my style? As long as I am doing my best most of the time and can let things happen as they happen and then do the best I can with them, I am perfectly human, and that is a supreme achievement. The alternative is hubris: "I can always get it right; I am better than other people." Enlightenment is ordinariness loved, *amor fati*. It is saying: "I let go of more than any fate can take."

Error and errancy are not tragedies. They are ingredients of and directions to discovery. They show us paths that humble us, startle us, and point us to new horizons. They do not have to lead to regret or shame. We say yes to our imperfection and accept our mistakes. We learn not to do it that way next time. Mistakes are not a sign of stupidity. They are human ways of learning. Recalling our big mistakes in life is a way of staying humble, the virtuous flower that blooms from the bud of yes. Humility leads us to commit ourselves to admitting our mistakes and making amends for anything we have done that may have hurt others. Such humility is a bridge to the letting go of regret.

Only the ego makes mistakes. None of our faults, crimes, or ignorant choices affect the stainless purity of our higher Self, our buddha nature, our Christ consciousness—or any conceptualization we use to describe the larger life in us that transcends ego. That life beyond conditions remains sane and infallible in us all our lives. It is accessed in moments of mindfulness and compassion. It cannot be usurped by anyone or anything. This reliable inner life is a form of protection and makes for an immense trust in our basic goodness. This is another way that the conditions of existence lead to the joy of spiritual maturity.

Things are not always as we would like them to be, nor do plans always work out our way. The fact that we are not in control means that the proper bearing for life on the raft of this world is surrender to what is as it is, how it is, when or where it is. We can fight with all our might for what can be changed, but only surrender works with what cannot be changed. The fact that we are not in control and that things happen that we neither sought nor planned means that there are forces at work bigger than our egos. This given is thus an intimation of divinity, as Emerson says: "So nigh is grandeur to our dust."

What is the divine? Something—we know not what or whom, we know not how or when—that is always at work, but we do know why: so we can fulfill our destiny to become unique exemplars of love and wisdom. The divine is the life force of the living universe that yearns to articulate itself in all of us. The finite is a unique moment of focus on the timeless infinite. We exist because of a beatific vision: The divine is focusing into time and space, and we are focusing back. When the divine arrives here, it is I, and when it reaches there, it is you, and when it lands outside my window, it is that fig tree under which Buddha was enlightened, sitting quietly in an attitude of yes for a long time.

NATURE'S DESIGN

The central plan of the whole universe is evolution. Everything is co-operating over time to make the world a more hospitable habitat for all creatures. The plan of nature is a model for us who are learning the word *yes*. Nature allows changes and flows with them. Nature is patient and nonretaliatory. Nature is fully respectful of interconnections. Nature honors the light and the dark.

Ecologist Thomas Berry writes: "Our new sense of the universe is itself a type of revelatory experience. . . . The natural world is itself the primary . . . presence of the sacred, the primary moral value. . . . The human community becomes sacred through its participation in the larger planetary community." Since we are related to nature as part to whole, to be fully human is to be fully natural. The term *human nature* says it all. Saint Anthony of the Desert (nature in his very name) wrote: "My scripture is the world of created things, and any time I wish to read the word of God, the book is open before me." Here "the word of God" is a metaphor for human wholeness, possible for individuals only when they enter into a global consciousness.

"An inner wholeness presses its still unfulfilled claims upon us," wrote Emma Jung so beautifully. Wholeness is an urge in the psyche, a motivating force in human behavior. This urge is the basis of self-trust. It is also an indicator that we are not yet fully human, not yet fully realized. This is why evolution is a spiritual project. Evolution is about how the urge toward wholeness is fulfilled. Our spiritual practices, our yes to life's givens, and our virtuous choices are our contribution. None of this is entirely individual; we are engaged in a collective transformation of consciousness. Wholeness is the urge of the universe, after all.

Nature offers a guiding blueprint for the human journey toward wholeness, since it is not composed of individuals but is an ecology, that is, interdependent. The daily story of the cosmos presents the themes of every human life: beginnings, endings, losses and restorations, metamorphoses of light and shadow, predictable and unpredictable events, reliable laws and lawless quantum leaps. The Zen poet Basho says: "All who have achieved real excellence in any art possess one thing in common, a mind to obey nature, to be one with nature throughout the four seasons of the year." Individual plans are therefore secondary to the larger purposes of a flowing universe.

Since we are not merely passive inhabitants of nature but participants in it, the inner life of nature is the same as our own inner life. Alternatively, to feel one with nature is to be in contact with the authentic depth of our essential being, the archetype of divinity within, the life force of reality, love itself.

Here is a trinity: the natural world, the human psyche, and the divine essence—three aspects of one underlying and ubiquitous reality. This equation is not pantheism but a trust that the animating energy of our humanity is the same as that which drives the universe. Divinity is thus the lively depth of us and of the cosmos. This sense of the divine in all is how the psyche and its psychology, the soul and its spirituality, and nature and its tangibility can be appreciated as one mystical ratio: humanity is to nature is to divinity.

We usually react to the given that life does not follow our plans with an oppositional defiance—fear and desire, debate and blame. Our plaintive reactions may derive from our inflated ego that insists that everything go our way. This adds to our suffering. It is the opposite of humbly accepting earthly conditions as they are. To say yes to letting things unfold as they will takes humble surrender. Nature meets us here, since such humility makes us closer to the earth. The word *humility*, in fact, comes from the word *humus*. To be humble is not self-abasement or mere modesty. It is the virtue of tuning ourselves to reality. Humility is a yes to the earthly conditions that make life so difficult but at the same time so exciting. To see this combination of opposites with some amusement makes things lighter and ultimately clearer. It is a useful practice to look for the humor in any given we encounter.

Humility is also the virtue that helps us when the given of life we face is that of powerlessness. For instance, when our young-adult son is on drugs, we remain available to support his recovery and we look for support for ourselves, but our unconditional yes is to our powerlessness. That takes ego reduction and letting go, for which humility is the recipe.

The conditions of existence are our open sesames to evolution: The given that life does not go according to plan makes the planet evolve in ways that humans could not devise quite so well. Thus nature reflects the identity and destiny of the human psyche as our model, our guide, and our twin, since nature and our psyche operate on the basis of the same axioms. Neither traits nor descriptions of me can exhaust my identity. I am more than can be sounded, counted, or known.

Nature—and we—join to say yes unconditionally to an expanded version of the five givens. Here is a list that shows what the givens of our lives look like when they happen in and to nature. Evolution is nature's plan, but it is not quite knowable. There is an order and balance in our universe that coexists with a formidable unpredictability beyond human control.

In the givens that follow ask yourself how each of them applies to your present way of living your life:

- Everything changes and passes from one form to another.
- Matter, like spirit, is not created or destroyed, but evolves in transformational seasons of beginning, growing, cresting, harvesting, dying, and renewing.
- The universe, like the human soul, is both finite and infinite.
- There is no single reliable configuration of how things are or how they are supposed to be or how they will turn out. Instead, there is infinite and unending possibility, just what animates our own souls.
- Events do not always line up in accord with the human version of order.
- Nothing and no one is truly separate; all is intricately and necessarily interconnected.
- Everything is zealously engaged in becoming what it is. Everything is becoming what it is meant to become no matter what the interferences or odds.
- Nothing is ever complete or finished. Everything is a work in progress, especially ourself.
- All beings in nature are subject to time by reason of birth and death.
- We are all continually evolving—taking on the new and letting go of the old—to fit the changing conditions of the environment. We evolve because of birth *and* death.
- The past of things and people strongly influences their present condition, yet it does not have to determine their future.
- Love, wisdom, and healing endure as driving forces both in our human stories and in the story of the universe. Simultaneously, nature is driven by destructive forces that are necessary for the survival of us all.
- When we intuit a truth of the universe, we feel a bodily resonance: It "feels right." We are clicking into the archetypal code of our humanity, and it matches the evolutionary code of the universe.
- The center of both the universe and the psyche is a single movable feast, and the circumference is nowhere to be found.

OUR CALLING

This is the true joy in life: being used for a purpose recognized by yourself as a mighty one, being thoroughly worn out before you are thrown on the scrap heap, being a force of nature instead of a feverish, selfish, little clod of ailments and grievances complaining that the world will not devote itself to making you happy.

—George Bernard Shaw

Our universal calling as humans is to be the most loving people we can be. This commitment makes us less likely to be at the mercy of others' reactions to us or opinions of us. We appreciate acceptance but do not crave or cling to it. We are hurt by rejection but not devastated by it. Our focus is on how we love, not on how we are loved, on how we can give, not on what we can get. What a loss to the world it would be if we lived our lives and neglected to activate fully our wondrously wide capacity to love!

Our calling is also about other capacities, gifts that are givens of who we are. Our life purpose is not simply to chop wood and carry water, as a Zen description of our tasks in life is sometimes interpreted. That plan is static, not evolutionary. Each of us is here to discover and share marvelously unique inner gifts. That is what the world is waiting for and why we were given a lifetime. Our appreciation of our gifts is itself the antidote to the self-loathing and self-diminution that we sometimes suffer.

Purpose is a direction based on design. Evolution has a direction and a purpose. For instance, a flower moves toward blossoming so that seeding can occur and it can return next spring. Likewise, the purpose of a caterpillar is a butterfly. There seems to be an orderly intrinsic directedness in all of nature, and certainly in us. We do not need an order or set of directions imposed on us by authority. Everything is heading into what it is meant to become. When we give up seeking the safety of control, order, and infallible rules, we find our bodily creativity, and then, once again, an axis of little ego and big

mind, an incarnation, happens. We become the word of life pro-
nounced in poetry and sculpted in light.

Abraham Maslow says that self-actualizing people are fascinated
by mystery. They do not avoid it in favor of clarity and certainty. This
is another feature of personal depth. Mystery honors the incompre-
hensible depth that resides in every finite reality. We can feel drawn
to the mystery of how the world works, to what underlies what we
see, and to what comes next in history, ours and the world's. This is
an attraction to what is emerging. Teilhard de Chardin spoke admir-
ingly of a "mysterious sense of the future . . . an attraction to the future as an organism progressing to the unknown." We feel drawn to
emergent properties of earth and ourselves that fit no categories yet
discovered. We futurists may find that we are upstarts not quite at
home in structures, institutions, or limited worldviews. We feel immortal evolutionary longings in the midst of change and end. Perhaps
those longings are the wake of the ferry called Divine Plan.

Evolved people realize that explanations of human events by
purely physical or purely psychological configurations cannot exhaust
their meaning. As long as nothing is more real than our mind, there
is no possibility of believing in a transcendent reality, not even within
us. For us intrepid explorers of inner seas of yes, there always remains
a hidden inner realm of mystery, a noumenon behind all phenomena.

The noumenon is the nonduality—the buddha mind or Christ
consciousness—that underlies and upholds all things. It is akin to the
nondual, object-free awareness arising in meditation. It is Being toward which beings are tensed but from which they are pulled by fear
and desire. Both attachment and avoidance keep us one step removed
from the edge of Being, toward which our individual being is spiritually tensed. Teilhard de Chardin described this invisible mystery of
Being as "the diaphany of the divine at the heart of the universe." I
take that to be somehow akin to scientist David Bohm's implicate
order beneath the surface of the explicate world.

To say there is such a transcendent reality behind appearances is to
say there is no split anywhere except in our landlubber minds. All that
is continually reveals itself to be the same as who we are. The Upanishads proclaim just such a larger life, nondually, diaphanously, im-

plicitly in us: "This supreme unborn spirit of humankind, unaging and undying, is the same as the spirit of the universe, and this realization is our refuge from every fear." With Hamlet, we fear "the slings and arrows of outrageous fortune." But fear vanishes once we realize there is no outside from which they can be aimed.

Insisting that things be different is a cause of suffering. Perhaps the *Rubáiyát of Omar Khayyám* misses the point when it laments the way things are in favor of the life we might remold. Our heart's desire might make a land of ice cream when woodenheads like us are called to be swallowed by a whale to become real. The more we notice that the universe does not respect our wishes, the more important is it for us to design a program to handle whatever may happen. That program is an unconditional yes to whatever is, was, or will be.

> *Would but some winged Angel ere too late*
> *Arrest the yet unfolded Roll of Fate,*
> *And make the stern Recorder otherwise*
> *Enregister, or quite obliterate!*
>
> *Ah, Love! could you and I with Him conspire*
> *To grasp this sorry Scheme of Things entire,*
> *Would not we shatter it to bits—and then*
> *Re-mould it nearer to the Heart's Desire!*
> *—The Rubáiyát of Omar Khayyám*
> (TRANSLATED BY EDWARD FITZGERALD)

THE LARGER LIFE

We are exploring the second given—that things don't always go according to plan—but in what follows I look at the matrix of all of our givens so we can see our subject in context:

EVERYTHING CHANGES AND ENDS evokes the archetype of renewal, shown in the mythic theme of resurrection. To let go of having things remain the same, to be open to change, to accept the varieties of human predicaments as fully legitimate, is rebirth into a spiritual world. The fact of renewal is itself an antidote to despair, a foundation for our belief that we never give up on the potential for redemption in anything or anyone.

THINGS DO NOT ALWAYS GO ACCORDING TO PLAN evokes the archetype of synchronicity, which reveals itself in a felt meaningful coincidence. To say yes to this given is to trust that the universe has a plan for us and that things are unfolding in this life just in time for us to grow into the beings we were meant to be. This is the Buddhist concept of karma as meaningful coincidence. Our own plans are based on our limited knowledge. The fact that things happen beyond our control and lead us to new vistas means that grace has come into play. This is the spiritual energy that cooperates in our expansion and arouses our imagination. We find room for more than our personal plans. We are stirred by ideals and aspirations that show us a path to transcending ego. It is a powerful evolutionary drive toward more and more light, that is, more and more enlightened consciousness on the planet.

There is such unity in the purposes of the universe and of ourselves that our very aspirations are indications of the direction of evolution. Our deepest needs, values, and wishes are not anomalous self-generated ideals. They are how the universe aims and achieves its evolutionary thrust. The universe needs us to expand its consciousness. This is why our highest spiritual accomplishment is to participate in evolution.

LIFE IS NOT ALWAYS FAIR is the archetype of karma as a consequence of dark choices, with the possibility of atonement and forgiveness in their train. When we accept the inadequacies of human justice, we accept the archetypal shadow, the dark side of life, events, and people. This dark side resides in all of us and thrives on projection of evil onto others and disavowal of it in ourselves. The shadow is a given of people and institutions. We are naive if we expect only integrity, justice, and love. We are lost if we cease to work for them with all our heart.

The bad breaks that happen in every life lead us to discover the felt meaning of karma, that all actions have consequences, some impossible to anticipate. We pronounce the unconditional and mindful yes best when we accept that all is as it needs to be, a series of intriguingly unpredictable karmic causes and effects. Karma is another example of interconnectedness. When we acknowledge the utter appropriateness of all that happens to us, we finally see the beauty of it and feel the safety in it. Nothing can happen to us that is not part of the story of ourselves, part of who we are and are becoming. We gradually see the meaningful coincidences by which the universe is acting in a purposeful way no matter how our own plans may be faring. We cease grumbling and accept reality just as it is, trusting that to be precisely the configuration that can move us on. Once we believe in connectedness, we sense no division between ourselves and what happens to us. That is the basis of our trust.

PAIN IS PART OF LIFE evokes the archetype of redemption. As long as we endure necessary suffering and dispel self-generated suffering, we are being redeemed, that is, revalued at a higher value than ego can pay, free of fear and open to love's challenges. To be reconciled to life as it is, no longer as a plaintiff, is how we find this redemption. To be redeemed is to be saved from being stopped or driven by fear or desire. We feel fear and desire as givens of life. Yet, through our trusting that there is a meaning in our suffering, we are no longer at the mercy of fear and desire. We can feel afraid and unsatisfied but not have to be driven or stopped as a result. Notice how often the word *trust* comes up in our discussion of the conditions of existence. Trust helps us find encouragement no matter how dark the givens may become.

PEOPLE ARE NOT LOVING AND LOYAL ALL THE TIME evokes the archetype of unconditional love. The "people" are our parents, our partners, our family, friends, and everyone in our lives. We can grow from the pain that happens in our relationships. We learn to become stronger. We do not give up on others. We make allowances for others' mistakes. We do not let others trample us down, but we do go on loving them. We dare to love no matter what. Our love is unconditional, but at the same time, our commitment to what we will do for others is wisely calibrated in accord with our own boundaries and limits.

We see the perfection of all that is, and we rest serenely in it. That is the equivalent of finding a holding environment, a reliable sanctuary that is able to contain all that we are and feel. Containment in childhood meant being held safely, soothed protectively, and understood empathetically by our parents. Such containment fosters a coherent and protective context for our maturing selves. Healthy relationships offer that same gift. This imitates the containment mother nature offers to conduct us to spiritual maturity. Wordsworth describes the protecting power of nature:

> Nature . . . can so inform
> The mind that is within us . . .
> that neither evil tongues . . .
> nor the sneers of selfish men . . .
> Shall e'er prevail against us, or disturb
> Our cheerful faith that all which we behold
> Is full of blessings.

IT ALL BALANCES IN LOVE

Our personal plans work best when they align with a larger plan. This happens when we live not only for ourselves and our loved ones but for the world as well. Loving-kindness fosters this responsiveness to a universal caring. We extend our concern beyond our immediate circle to a universe without circumference. Nature does this too, in that it tailors each species to support others. Shakespeare reminds us in *The Merchant of Venice* that "such harmony is in immortal souls," and loving-kindness is a purposeful expression of it.

The balance of nature is not always harmonious, however. It includes room for occasional confusion and disorder. We notice that same chaos in our own lives, no matter how devoted we are to spiritual practices and how earnestly we do our psychological work. Yet there is something in us, too, something that is never spent and that irrepressibly survives the tumult of life. This something is the energy that contains us and the universe. This life force, the most reassuring given, is something that endures in us, through us, and beyond us, un-damaged and integral, no matter what may have happened to us in the course of our lives.

We make the effort to engage in spiritual practices, and then shifts follow that take us beyond the limitations of our ego. These shifts are supplemental graces, personified by the assisting forces in the hero stories. In most tales, the hero or heroine performs his or her task only with the aid of kindly forces, as, for example, Dorothy was helped by the scarecrow, the tin man, and the lion. This is another example of how interconnectedness is such a necessary ingredient for human growth. Assisting forces turn the scared ego into a champion of love, the ignorant ego into a mentor of wisdom, the broken ego into a mir-acle worker. Nature then holds the ego tenderly, and the ego relaxes and lets itself be held. That is the felt meaning and promise of a bal-ance of person and world, of ego and archetype, of human and divine energies. The ego always wanted to be held like this, no matter how fierce its kicking and screaming.

There are balances we cannot effect or even imagine but that hap-pen when love takes us one step beyond fear. The reason love casts out fear is that love creates the feeling of safety. When we act with love, we feel so good about ourselves that courage blooms. We find the poise to be at home with givens that scared us before. They bless us with the gifts of the unconditioned universal Self: believing in our powers and being comfortable with them, letting go of control, prac-ticing loving-kindness, surrendering to this startling moment, daring defiantly to break through the gates that say "Keep out" or "Don't go beyond this point."

May I trust the forces that help me know who I am and where I am going, and may all those who doubt themselves and disregard their destiny likewise be surrounded by in-escapable evidence of their limitless identity and destiny.

THREE

LIFE IS NOT ALWAYS FAIR

The Law of life lives in him with his unreserved consent.
— MIRCEA ELIADE

LIFE IS not always fair and neither are people, ourselves included. Sometimes we are taken advantage of. Sometimes we do all the right things and wind up losing. Sometimes we act cautiously and are nonetheless hurt. Others may be generous to us and yet we take advantage of their kindness. Or we may act with good intentions toward others and yet our efforts go unappreciated or are misinterpreted. The third given challenges our ability to grieve for the losses associated with unfairness. This is our psychological work. It also challenges us not to retaliate against those who have hurt us. This is our spiritual practice. Both these together equal an unconditional yes to the unalterable law that things are not always fair: You win some; you lose some.

The challenge is to meet our losses with loving-kindness, the commitment to act and think lovingly toward others, especially when they test our patience or act hurtfully toward us. Cultivating loving-kindness when people treat us unfairly or hurtfully helps us by keeping our hearts open in and through the moment of being hurt. Openness does not mean we let ourselves be victims of abuse. We simply allow ourselves to be what we are at our most loving, that is, vulnerable. Any human interaction or relationship can have painful moments in it. A mature adult notices that closing off is dangerous to her sensitivity and that remaining too open is dangerous to her boundaries. The middle path means a willingness to be open while also maintaining healthy boundaries. We can commit ourselves to that form of yes by a practice: We seek amends when others treat us unfairly, ask for redress, and if this doesn't work, we let go, and our hearts do not close. Letting go has the effect of opening the heart.

REVENGE OR RECONCILE?

It is a given of the gene pool *Homo sapiens* to live on the default setting of retaliation. It takes a spiritual practice to override this natural impulse. We have to customize our ego and undo the factory settings. The primitive ego's favorite sport, retaliation, is the opposite of not giving up on others. To take revenge opposes the teachings of the buddhas and saints. What is the spiritual practice that works? It is loving-kindness: a mindful yes, compassion, understanding, a belief that all humans are redeemable, and a commitment to reconciliation. Loving-kindness frees us from the retaliatory instinct of ego.

If I accept you as you are without protest or blame, I am not driven to get back at you as your judge or executioner. I am a fair and alert witness who sees unfairness but does not punish the unfair. Instead I speak up and at the same time work for the transformation of the unjust. It is a spiritual practice to notice others' behavior without having to criticize them about it or get back at them for it. That spiritual practice has a power that effects transformation in others.

To reconcile instead of retaliate leads to closeness between the wounded and wounding parties. Usually we run from conflict, just as we run from closeness. Dialogue is the alternative to withdrawal or retribution. An adult knows that losses will happen sometimes, that unfair dealings will sometimes occur, and that he can survive them. A spiritually evolved adult is not satisfied with the glee of retaliation but wants the joy of loving-kindness. This happens when we act in accord with the standards of love. It happens when we do not fall into a despair about others that is the true origin of revenge. Despair is a loss of our sense of connectedness.

A spiritual practice is required because psychological goals cannot morally motivate us. It takes moral consciousness to forgive those who are not sorry for how they have offended us. We cannot plan to forgive or make ourselves forgiving. It happens when we commit ourselves to nonretaliation. We feel healthy anger about how others mistreated us. We may even speak up and report the impact of the offense on us, but then we let go of blame and the need to punish. This is the direct result of the vow we can make at any time to cease retaliating.

Sometimes people admit their guilt and show contrition. The healthy psyche is inherently geared to release compassion when it sees pain and defeat, just as it releases forgiveness when it sees repentance. Repentance is contrition, amends, and a commitment not to repeat the offense. In the face of that response in an offender, our instinct is to forgive. This requires no practice. When we see penitence that is genuine, we are calibrated to forgive automatically. What makes us not show compassion or feel forgiveness is falling prey to our mean-spirited ego, which drugs our nobler innate instinct. Shakespeare explains this in *The Tempest*:

> Though with their high wrongs I am struck to
>   the quick,
> Yet with my nobler reason against my fury
> Do I take part: the rarer action is
> In virtue than in vengeance: they being
>   penitent,
> The sole drift of my purpose doth extend
> Not a frown further.

Retaliation does not balance things, since it harms the soul of the retaliator and creates a more severe imbalance. Socrates noticed this peril and wrote: "It is better to suffer an injustice than to commit one." This is because the body and mind are damaged by injustice from others, but it is our own soul that is damaged by revenge. A spiritually evolved adult is not cutthroat and does not believe that all is fair in love and war. He does not claw his way to the top but acts kindly at any rung of the ladder. He has personal ambition but not at the expense of others. This is an example of a moral standard becoming more important than success in the material world. The joy of a good conscience is the highest value for those who want to grow spiritually. With spiritual practice, our attitude toward an aggressor becomes compassion for the *suffering* dimension in his aggression. This response also serves to quiet him down. In the martial art of aikido, the point is not to harm the opponent but to redirect and transform his or her aggression, ultimately bringing the opponent to the realization that violence does not work. Finding an alternative to violence is a way of awakening and a joyous way to feel one's authentic power.

In an evolved society, animated by spiritual consciousness, the desire for retribution is replaced with the desire for restoration. We want to reconcile, not excommunicate. In such a world—sadly, not this one yet—everyone is accountable and is asked to make amends, but no one is punished, since restoration is how satisfaction is truly made. *In my personal life, do I live in the precivilized world of revenge or the new, admittedly smaller, world of forgiving and restorative love?*

Retribution aims at	*Restoration moves toward*
• Punishing the evildoer as evil	• Seeking to heal the ignorance of the "evildoer"
• Satisfying society's need for revenge	• Harmony
• Making someone pay	• Having someone make amends
• Getting even	• Caring that a fallen brother or sister find redemption
• Getting rid of a disturbing and dangerous presence	• Correcting and then reincluding

- Guaranteeing the safety of society at the cost of causing the aggressor to suffer, with no chance at rehabilitation

- Guaranteeing the safety of society while being compassionate to the aggressor's pain and helping the person recover his or her humanity

- Preserving the historical style of dealing with injustice (an eye for an eye)

- Finding an exciting and more humanitarian solution to injustice

- Imagining and wishing Hitler in hell for all the evil he perpetrated and for which he will never be forgiven

- Imagining Hitler in a Zen monastery, where a strict but wise abbot is pointing to his deeds and teaching him to ask for forgiveness until he becomes an enlightened buddha and comes back to help humanity

- Maintaining the either . . . or belief in a hell (eternal) or heaven

- Generating a belief only in purgatory or rebirth (temporary) and heaven or nirvana

- Making sure the cycle of retaliation continues so that war can be justified

- Ending the cycle of retaliation so that war will no longer be an acceptable solution

- End of story

- Beginning of a dialogue

Our unconditional yes to the given of unfairness is twofold. We acknowledge the unfairness others enact without the need to retaliate. We acknowledge that our society is still too primitive to have a court system or a government that seeks restoration instead of retribution by capital punishment and war. Since we do not give up on others or on society, we never stop looking for a way to change things for the better.

If someone treats us unfairly in our personal life, the challenge is to make sure something changes in our relationship—not to make sure the person is punished. The former plan comes from a wish for healing. The latter comes from the dark tendency of the bruised ego to hurt back.

We are noticing a difference in the given of unfairness from the other four givens. Here our unconditional yes includes work to alter the fact. In the others we accept by accepting; in this one we accept and also work with all our might for a change. Yes is surrender as alignment. This means doing all we can to align our personal and public policies to the ideals of reconciliation and nonviolence.

Imagine the mature spiritual consciousness that produced the following poem by Shantideva, an eighth-century Indian Buddhist teacher:

> May those whose hell it is
> To hate and hurt
> Be turned into lovers
> Bringing flowers.

Instead of saying that those who hate and hurt belong in hell, he notices with compassion that it must feel like hell to hate and hurt others. Instead of wishing that those who hate or hurt be punished, he prays for their transformation. Instead of wishing they be turned into toads, he wants them to become lovers who have found happiness and are sharing it generously. To let go of the fire and brimstone that may have characterized our religious past is to become a lover, awakening in heaven on earth.

WHY DOES HARM COME TO THE INNOCENT?

The perennial human conundrum is, "Why do the innocent suffer?" Implicit in that question is that the guilty should suffer; they should be punished. Retaliation is so deeply imprinted in our collective psyche that we expect it as a guarantee. Usually this expectation applies to others more than to ourselves. Our ego demands that we be "let off easy" and may be enraged when we are required to pay for our offenses.

Another way the collective imprint of retaliation shows itself is in our own pervasive sense of guilt. The Latin word for "to be sorry"—*poenitere*—is related to the Latin word for punishment—*poena*. From ancient times a connection has been made between doing wrong and being punished for it. Authorities and patriarchies take advantage of that built-in belief to keep us under their control. We internalize the fear that reprisals will automatically come our way if we do something wrong. We feel a gnawing and unremitting sense that we have done wrong and not been fully punished for it, so we are waiting for the sword of Damocles to drop on our heads. This is a superstitious belief in retaliation by the angry gods. It is part of the primitive heritage of our collective humanity.

Punishment is a form of superstition in the sense that it is apotropaic, an attempt to ward off evil by a ritual. Yet spiritual consciousness helps us admit and permit our inner opposites, not as dichotomies, but as complementaries. For all our demands of fairness, the innocent suffer nonetheless, and the guilty suffer too. The innocent experience happiness and so do the guilty. Every religion promises a happy ending to the human story. Yet the God on the ceiling of the Sistine Chapel is not making sure things all come out even.

I can't forget a touching statement on a card I received many years ago. It was written by a Catholic monk and pictured Jesus saying, "For you the hill slants more. The cross is of a heavier weight. But do not be discouraged, for when you seem to suffer most, remember that then we are most truly companions." The question about why God permits suffering changes as a more mature religious consciousness emerges. Then we know that God suffers too. This is because what we have called God is not a separate supreme being looking down on us from his invincible and impassible height. Rather, God may be the deepest ground and reality of all beings. The words of the Roman poet Terence fit for God too: "Nothing human is alien from me." We might have noticed that in the image of Jesus on the cross. In the archetypal view, the suffering God is suffering because God suffers, not because we made God suffer. Friedrich Nietzsche comments: "The gods justified human life by living it themselves—the only satisfactory theodicy ever invented." *The real—and exciting—mystery is not why God permits suffering but "What evolutionary power must suffering have if even God shares in it?"*

In an immature spiritual consciousness we might pray: "Save me from the givens of life." In a mature spiritual consciousness we pray: "Be with me in the givens so I can handle them. Stay with me in them rather than abrogate them for me. I don't want to miss out on all they can teach me."

THE ART OF TAMING EGO

He rifles through my secret store
The Saracen of buzz
His greedy love a scimitar
That pries my pollens free.

So I, undone, unloose my gown
And flourish low a bow
To welcome in his rowdy fuzz
And let myself be stung.

— DAVID RICHO

Our ego is indignant about its having to kowtow to conditions that do not safeguard its entitlement to fame, fortune, health, happiness, and invincibility. This neurotic ego is not an identity but a set of encrustations: Fear, Attachment, Control, Entitlement. This is the FACE we keep trying to save and will do anything not to lose. These are the four motives of the driven ego and the cause of our suffering. We save face and lose heartfulness. And the upkeep the ego requires can be exhausting.

The FACE of ego can be transformed with spiritual commitment. Fear can be replaced with love. Attachment can turn into letting go. Control can soften into allowing. Entitlement can become working for justice without hate or retaliation. This face-lifted ego no longer hates anyone. Hate is not in the repertory of a healthy person, neither psychologically nor spiritually.

The ego is a wild horse that can be tamed by a higher consciousness, by buddha mind, the blissful state of awareness and openness, of nondual consciousness, that is our true nature. At some point the broncobuster of enlightenment shows it cannot be unseated and is here to stay. At that moment the high horse of ego realizes it is fighting against its own life purpose: "My inability to win shows me this is who I am and what I was meant for. This is why I have a back like this. So let me be ridden." Now they work together as allies.

Our ego was never meant to die, only to be tamed so that its wild energies could be put to better use. Its FACE can change: The energy in its fear becomes excitement about challenges and caution about dangers. The energy in its attachment becomes commitment. The energy in its control becomes the ability to get things done. The energy in its entitlement becomes a healthy sense of justice that works indefatigably for what is right but never stoops to retribution as a solution.

All this requires the dismantling of the neurotic ego so that the healthy ego may thrive. How can we facilitate this transition? It takes a tenfold yes. As a spiritual practice, do a searching inventory of yourself about each of the ten listings that follow. How true are they of you? Rewrite them as affirmations if that helps:

- We become utterly transparent, no longer trying to look good.
- We accept rather than oppose any condition of existence, no matter how minor; for example, we patiently wait in line at the checkout stand instead of huffing and puffing. A more weighty example might be our acceptance of the death of a child. Grief includes sadness and anger but does mean that we become bitter or suicidal.
- We act justly in our own dealings and work for justice in society.
- We do not lose sight of the essential humanity of those who do evil things, never giving up on others' transformation. This is an implication of impermanence. No matter how badly someone may have

acted, she can change for the better, so we never give up. We forgive others and look for ways to reconcile.

- We drop the expectation of permanence in anything at all, for example, absolute integrity in ourselves or fairness from others.
- We acknowledge our own dark side. We admit our wrongs—present and past—and make amends. This helps us let go of regrets and keeps us humble.
- We feel compassion for the innocent who suffer, dropping the why if it is a natural disaster, asking why if it is human created.
- We do not hate.
- We cease seeking to be perfect but want only to be faithful to our psychological work and our spiritual practice.
- We see the givens of life as moments that present us a gift and a door. We are thankful and we cross the threshold.

COMMITMENTS BEYOND EGO

The human brain contains our entire evolutionary history. According to neuroscientist Paul MacLean, our brain can be understood as having three levels: reptilian, mammalian, and cognitive-rational. We can think of the instinctive reptilian core of our brain as establishing our sense of agency and action in a world that can be either nurturing or threatening, allowing us to react with discernment. This level of our brain is concerned with survival. Our mammalian brain gives us a sense of our being-with-others and with all of nature. This level is where society and cooperation begin. Our cerebral cortex, or "human brain," can give us a sense of linking to a world beyond the fraying strands of time. This is where the intellectual, imaginative, and spiritual are born and thrive.

When our ego is caught in fear, we do not access our mammalian sense of belonging and all the wonderful potential it offers for cooperation. Instead we may operate from our reptilian past and break our connection with others or even become violent. This stunts the growth of our full humanity, a gift to us that it has taken nature many millennia to grant. We sometimes live as if only survival were real, as if our only resources were reptilian. That is where war, retaliation, and aggression take the reins. As humans we are inherently loving, but fear can prevent that love from arising. Then only our fierce warrior archetype is allowed to flourish and not the kindly steward archetype. That is dangerous, since it is an abridgement of ourselves, a patch from the full fabric of our nature. It is a conditional yes to who we are.

A commitment to nonviolence and virtue is one that only a minority of people make—another given, that so few people make such a commitment? It is not the style of the mainstream; it is peripheral in society and government. A mindful yes to the given that so few people are nonviolent leads to fewer expectations and a cessation of blame of others. To acknowledge the power of the dark side of collective humanity means that war comes as no surprise. Our spiritual consciousness arises in our protest and in our compassion for those who do not yet believe in the possibilities of peaceful solutions. We say yes to the fact that we are a minority. We do this without despairing, since we have not given up on the emergence of a newer world in the making.

The collective shadow of humanity includes war, genocide, slavery, retaliation, racism, scapegoating, and torture. The tendency of this negative shadow to take over human affairs is proportional to how decadent a society has become. In the "both . . . and" spirit, we say yes to these hard facts, rather than deny them. At the same time, we never give up on working for change, while knowing all along that perfect goodness will never fully prevail. War is a given of this gene pool but one that could be reversed at any time if we were to choose to do so. Or do we have to wait for the departure of *Homo sapiens* and the arrival of *Homo spiritualis*?

Our spiritual practice of yes is the paradox of paradoxes and the miracle of miracles. This is because we are the living—though at times endangered—proof that the primitive shadow inclinations of the human collective can be defied and steadily evolve. We are indeed the only chance for its survival. We act with nonviolent love not because it is a strategy that works every time but because it is who we are beyond ego.

A MINDFUL REPLY TO UNFAIRNESS

We can extend mindfulness into our day by noticing the FACE of our ego at work in our fears, our attachments—the preferences we cling to—our tendencies to control others, and our sense of entitlement. We then simply label them as causes of suffering without shame or revulsion. Such equanimity, awareness, and acceptance is a remedy to the fundamental unsatisfactoriness of human life (the first noble truth of Buddhism). Likewise, in mindfulness, "to do" and "to be" meet felicitously and become one experience.

Unfairness is about breaking a connection of trust. Mindfulness leads to compassion, so mindfulness, like early development and adult intimacy, is about connectedness. It may seem that mindfulness is a solo activity and therefore not related to the interconnectedness of all beings. Yet in an engaged mindfulness meditation we attend to our breath not as ours only but as one with the breath of all beings and things. We are breathing in the air that all of us share now and have breathed before. We are breathing not as individuals but as participants in the universe that is breathing through us. Every spiritual practice is about everything, once the scared ego is no longer at the helm.

Daily meditation and mindfulness lead to liberation from imprisonment in the citadel of ego in favor of a freewheeling life of wisdom and compassion. Indeed, mindfulness is a liberating wisdom because it reveals to us the true FACE of our neurotic ego. Since this is the same face our fellow humans are also trying to save, we feel compassion for them. Mindfulness becomes a yes to love.

Mindfulness as a meditation practice means sitting daily for at least fifteen minutes focusing on our breathing. When the mind-sets of ego—fear, desire, judgment, plans, fantasies—interrupt, we gently return our attention to the here-and-now reality of our breath. This is mindfulness as a yes to the present moment.

By a mindful yes we contact the something in us—the buddha mind, Christ consciousness, higher power—that is not hounded by fairness or unfairness, gain or loss, success or failure, fame or oblivion,

plenty or paucity, praise or blame, pleasure or pain, joy or sorrow, reward or punishment, life or death.

Our commitment to accept the present just as it is, to permit its full
career, and to live in it fully turns givens into graces. Changes and
endings become visions of the reality of impermanence so we can let
go more easily. Plans falling through awaken us to the mystery of synchronicity. A lack of fairness makes us more zealous to work for justice. The suffering in ourselves leads us to be compassionate to the
suffering in others. The disloyalty or lovelessness of others gives us
the gift of tears and turns us more intensely to our practice of loving-
kindness. Our unconditional yes to the present makes it a present
opened.

*May I be fair in all my dealings and generous in all my giv-
ing, and may I ask for fairness from others but not demand
it or punish them if they fail to show it to me.*

FOUR

PAIN IS PART OF LIFE

*For our heart to yield without revolt to the hard law of cre-
ation, is there not a psychological need to find some positive
value that can transfigure this painful waste in the process
that shapes us and eventually make it worth accepting? . . .
Dark and repulsive though it is, suffering has been revealed
to us as a supremely active principle for the humanization
and the divinization of the universe.*
— Pierre Teilhard de Chardin

A given of life is that there is a cost to everything, and suffering is
part of that cost. This given is stated in the first noble truth of Buddhism, which is often translated into English as "Life is suffering," or
"Life is unsatisfactory." Another way of stating this truth or given is
that *pain is not punishment, and pleasure is not reward.* They are simply
features of any existence.

We suffer physically, psychologically, and spiritually and we grow
in those same ways. Suffering seems to be an ingredient of growth
during every phase and on every threshold of our development. Yet
suffering is not a device used by some power in the sky to make us
grow. It is not a trip to the woodshed. It is not imposed but rather
built into the very nature of change, another mystery that the ego
keeps dismissing.

Physically, pain can happen acutely, by a sudden accident or a wound inflicted by someone. Pain can also be chronic and may not yield to treatments meant to alleviate it. Some physical pain is self-inflicted and can be a sign of a serious psychological disorder.

There are many kinds of psychological pain. We are all subject to mental distresses; mood problems or illnesses, including depression, anxiety, obsession, compulsion, character disorders; and addictions. Some psychological pain is the consequence of natural events that occur in every human life. This pain is aroused by losses, disappointments, betrayals, abandonments, malicious behavior, and so forth.

One example is the suffering we experience when a loss occurs. It is a given that in any enterprise or activity we stand to lose something. We can lose a partner, a parent, a child, a friend. We can be hurt or robbed while in our hometown or while traveling. We can lose in the stock market or lose at love or lose our heads. Not to be able to accept the pain in losses, reverses, endings, unfairness, or any other given is a disability. It will be hard to live happily if the laws of life cannot be taken in stride. The givens become causes of suffering when we insist on rejecting them or when we break down in the face of them. Anything but yes is a handicap.

Some people draw pain and crisis to themselves; some have it thrust upon them and make themselves feel more pain by how they react to it. We all have to face pain, and when we experience it mindfully, we simply feel it as it is. When we add the ego layers, the mindsets of fear, blame, shame, attachment to an outcome, complaint, or obsession, we make things worse.

Here is an example: I make a poor investment and lose money. The pain associated with such loss is grief. I add new and more ferocious dimensions to my sadness about the loss when I blame myself, call myself stupid, and keep obsessing about my mistake. I then try to control all future dealings with money more carefully than ever and become phobic about spending. Now I am caught in chains forged by my own mind. This is why letting go of ego is so crucial to liberation. It allows us to experience reality with its natural consequences, which are never as severe as the ones we devise in our heads. In addition, reality and its consequences are trustworthy synchronicities that lead us to new perspectives and possibilities. Could it be that all our mental gyrations are flights from reality and destiny?

There are some people who live life serenely free of crisis or great pain. Is this random or purposeful? Jung says: "There is no room for chance in the meaningful world of the psyche." Buddhism relates all events to an invisible order of karma. The Judeo-Christian and Islamic religions propose that there is meaning in a divine plan no matter how jumbled things may appear. Depth psychology sees all happenings as synchronous paths to find and live out our full potential.

Events happen to reveal the truth of what our life is about, a truth we try so hard to evade, cancel, or reverse. Yet, it is also a given that we will never understand why certain things happen. In fact, the comfort we derive from explanations makes us wonder about the authenticity of our explanations. Perhaps the need to know is part of the ego's demand that it be in control. That way of living does not accommodate the full range of mysteries we meet up with in life. A psychology or a religion that explains everything cuts us off from a sense of wonder about the world and from growth in humility about ourselves. Saint John of the Cross, a Spanish mystic, happily declared his spiritual predicament in this way: "I entered I knew not where, and there I stood not knowing: nothing left to know."

All the traditions seem to agree that meaningful growth comes at the price of pain. Why? That is a mystery, and the fact that there is no satisfying answer is related to the first noble truth of the pervasive unsatisfactoriness of human life. It can only be greeted with a yes, not deconstructed with a reply.

In Buddhism, karma is the basis of trusting what happens, of trusting the cards we are dealt, of trusting the pain we did not plan. Belief in karma requires trust that there is something afoot that ego does not conjure. This is perhaps the something we know not what, we know not how, that is always at work so that evolution can proceed and flourish through us. Something in our own reality is continually transfiguring us through our pain. Is this what is meant by joy in suffering?

It is said of pain that we will never be given more than we can bear.

An adult has accepted the given that no one is up there making sure of this. Indeed, Jung says: "Sometimes the divine asks too much of us." What we can bear is directly proportional to the inner strength and resources we have gathered in the course of life. A treasury of nature, poetry, art, music, love, spiritual integrity; a coherent sense of self; access to an adult version of a higher power; and our cherished relationships grant endlessly rich sources of nurturance.

Our capacity to deal with pain grows in accord with our spiritual practice and our psychological work. But even when we have worked on ourselves, there may still be events and moments that are too much. Humility lies in accepting reality with all its surprises and in accepting ourselves with all our limitations.

We learn to handle whatever happens to us not only through our work on ourselves. In childhood we attached ourselves and our trust to the caregivers who nurtured and protected us. Our parents watched out for us so that we did not have to face more than we could bear. They could not be successful every time, however. Safety for us as adults does not mean we will not be hurt or not die. It means we will accept the support of others and do all we can on our own and then allow life to unfold on its own terms.

Our attachment to wise guardian parents actually helped us learn to protect ourselves. Repeated safe-haven experiences led to a sense of internal safety: "Because you helped me handle things, I can now handle what happens to me." As healthy adults, we internalized the safe base modeled and granted by our caring parents. This sense of an inner reliable safety is what is meant by groundedness or centeredness. It is also what is meant by an inner sense of the presence of God or of Buddha as a refuge.

People who endure severe pain may suffer later from posttraumatic stress disorder. A striking exception has been observed in the Tibetans who have been tortured by the Chinese. They seem to recover relatively unscathed. During their ordeal, they remain centered in their practice of compassion for their oppressors and in their consciousness of working through karma. Tibetans are thereby saying yes to the harsh reality of their predicament in an egoless way. They do not retaliate later. They do not hate their persecutors. They experience an equanimity that lets them get on with life with love intact. What an argument this makes for the necessity of a spiritual practice if we are to survive in a healthy way!

ARE WE VICTIMS?

When God is seen as a rescuer or parent in the sky, we may depend on him for protection and lose our faith if he does not come through. When we give up the childhood version of life, we stand on our own, surrounded by others but not necessarily defended by them against life's disturbing threats. With no "parent" on the lookout, we notice that we sometimes have to bear more than we can handle, and we may fold under the pressure. This too requires a yes. Our purpose in life is not to remain upright at all times but to collapse with grace when that is what has to happen. The fact of impermanence gives us the hope that we will rise again.

Even the most daring hero is sometimes defeated and has to rely on others for rescue, others who may or may not come through successfully. Since life is a journey, we grow not only by conquest of fear but also by occasional surrender to it. Thus the fact that we are given more than we can bear at times is not a flaw in life or in us but one of the ways we fulfill ourselves by dismantling our ruggedly individualistic egos. We learn to rely on others, however inadequate, and thus acknowledge our interconnectedness. Recall Robin Hood in prison, shorn of his powers of derring-do, waiting for Maid Marion to come through.

The self-help movement sometimes insists, perhaps too rigidly, that we are never to be victims. An adult knows that being victimized is sometimes unavoidable in a full life experience. We all are taken advantage of sometimes, cheated at times, betrayed at times, deceived at times, down for the count at times. No matter how we try to avoid all these possibilities, no matter how fiercely we seek redress when they occur, we cannot dodge them fully. Every human archetype, including that of the victim, is legitimate at one time or another once we are humble enough to accept the fact that anything can happen to anyone. (This means letting it be quite all right to be anyone rather than insisting I am Somebody.)

To be human is to be vulnerable, and an ego that cannot accommodate that and move through it is a hazard to spiritual development. If everything collapses, I will deal with it by staying with the pieces and then picking up the pieces. That piecework practice helps us distinguish two kinds of victims: Some victims lay themselves open for pain and contempt. They may wait for someone to come along and set them free. They become more and more open to being preyed upon as they lose their boundaries.

Other victims, however, are simply vulnerable in an open, healthy way and let themselves experience the betrayals that life and relationship sometimes bring. They are hurt, but they have a spiritual technology to deal with their hurt. They do not hurt back. They do not let themselves be hurt more. They stand up for themselves and wish enlightenment for those who hurt them. This is how they let their hearts open more than ever and become strong against predators while still penetrable to the slings and arrows of love. They may be victims but they are not casualties.

Pain is personal sometimes. Someone says something to me that hurts my feelings. At other times it is bigger than any one person. Someone scapegoats or injures me because of my beliefs, race, or sexual preference. Such a hate crime harks back to the collective dark side of humanity.

No one human being can or is meant to deal with so dangerous a burden; one needs a community in which to hold it and handle it. Otherwise one feels terribly isolated and fragmented. Possession by the archetypal suffering of our race is too much for anyone, even a hero. For instance, someone might feel the impact of war or anti-Semitism so thoroughly as to be rendered immobile because of grief or driven to suicidal missions because of the fanatical wishes of others to eliminate them. Yet, "My desolation does begin to make a better life," says Cleopatra in Shakespeare's *Antony and Cleopatra*. We can work with our predicament and appreciate it as a path.

A spiritually evolved adult seeks not an answer but a significance.

This is because it is harder to bear what is undefined and what puzzles us. Mature meaning derives not necessarily from a clear understanding but from the opportunities for wisdom and compassion offered by the event. Grasping meaning is more a matter of appreciation than of intellectual certainty.

Here are three charmingly connected comments on meaning: "Meaning makes things endurable, perhaps everything," wrote C. G. Jung. This tells us we can say yes to whatever happens to us. The mystic saint Teresa of Ávila said: "When we accept what happens to us and make the best of it, we are praising God." So yes is a prayer that liberates and transforms us. The Hindu sage Govinda adds, "We are transformed by what we accept. We transform what we have accepted by understanding it." Thus the adult challenge is to believe that there is a design that wants to come through in our lives despite the random and untidy display. A yes that is mindful and unconditional is the telescope through which we see that design. Then we have the vision to behold a constellation instead of a stray array of straggling stars.

A YES TO THE PAIN NATURE BRINGS

Redemption is a separation and deliverance from an earlier condition of darkness and unconsciousness, and leads to a condition of illumination and victory over everything "given."

—C. G. JUNG

The story of the Buddha's enlightenment conveys to us the fact that pain and darkness are part of the natural order of things—and that nature is an ally in our work of facing the realities of life head-on. As the legend goes, after many years of spiritual searching, the Buddha sat in meditation under a bodhi tree vowing not to move from that spot until he gained enlightenment. As he sat there, the evil forces of Mara (an army of demons) attacked him.

In a Thai version of the story, the Buddha had been surrounded by congratulatory devas, kindly semidivine spirits. Yet they all fled instantly because of their fear of Mara. Only the earth goddess, Nang Thoranee, remained by Buddha's side. When Buddha touched her, that is, touched the earth, she rose before him as a beautiful woman. Remembering how Buddha had once made an offering of water to her, she wrung her wet hair so that torrents of water flooded the path of the invading armies. She then brought thunder and earthquakes to rout them completely. The dark side of the earth became a force of assistance in the form of natural disasters. The powers of darkness were not destroyed, only displaced. This acknowledges the shadow archetype that remains among us no matter how strongly we oppose it. The shadow is an unsupplantable given of life.

When the Buddha found enlightenment, the demons felt consternation at the prospect of so much light coming into the world. This is the archetype of the combination of opposites: Light arouses shadow and shadow arouses light. Goodness is attacked by evil forces, and forces of goodness battle forces of darkness.

The shadow is C. G. Jung's term for the dark side of the psyche, personified and embodied in individuals and in collective events in history. Our confusions and shadow impulses serve to make us more interesting to ourselves. Since nature partakes of consciousness, it too has a shadow side. It takes the forms of earthquakes, floods, volcanic eruptions, hurricanes, tornadoes, tsunamis, and so forth. Nature is not just flowers and bunnies; it contains some unpleasant and highly destructive elements. To love nature does not mean having to enjoy all its vicissitudes and moods. But it does mean honoring all the seasons and possibilities.

What form does the honoring take? It is the yes of simply accepting the painful or unappealing aspects of the natural world as necessary and ineluctable, no matter how distressing they may be. This is befriending the dark rather than fearing or hating it. We make a place for the mud, the slime, the venomous insects, the rats, the things and places that seem ugly to us, the odors and tastes that are unsavory to us, the unexpected events that terrify and harm us. "I watched the water snakes . . . no tongue their beauty might declare," Coleridge's

Ancient Mariner said in his moment of enlightenment. To be enlightened is to see light in the dark, another combination of opposites.

We can utter an unconditional, mindful yes to the varieties of light and dark in our planetary existence without complaint or hesitation. To maintain a split world, bad and good, means that, in consequence, we split ourselves into fear of one and desire for the other. To accept reality as integrated, containing all opposites and reconciling them, is to be free of the shackles of fear and desire. This is how psychological sanity and clarity can be occasions for awakening.

In Buddhism, and in many other religions, we encounter images of blissful and wrathful nature deities. These are personifications of the population of our inner life. They are not contradictory archetypes but represent the unified reality that has been so often divided by our analyzing minds. What do *blissful* and *wrathful* mean? They are subjective terms: When we are caught in ego, the archetypes of our inner life appear as wrathful; when we are mindful, they appear as blissful. They want to be our friends and they test our loyalty with their fearsomeness. Shadow figures that scare us become allies, because when we face them, they grant us their fearlessness. This happens when we are motivated by the affirmation yes rather than the question why.

BEING WITH THE SUFFERING OF OTHERS

Mindfulness meditation is meant to be a daily practice. There are two types of meditation we may consider. The first is called concentration meditation, in which we pay attention to one idea, object, or image in calm abiding, that is, not interrupted or driven by the mind-sets of ego such as fear or desire. The other is called mindfulness meditation, in which we do not concentrate on an external object but simply notice the minute-by-minute activity of our minds. We notice the ongoing chatter in our heads and realize how it can lead to our believing we are a separate self. We are indeed distinct beings, but when we fixate on that fact, we lose sight of the other truth about us—that we are interconnected and not ultimately separate in any fixed, final, or independent way. Mindfulness reveals our true nature in nature.

Psychology and spirituality continually coalesce. Jung noticed a positive dimension in the mental chatter that seems to become rampant during meditation: He saw it as a path to exploring the images and thoughts of the unconscious. The Buddha taught that we should live with mindful presence in the moment. Heinz Kohut, a psychologist of the Self, speaks of "empathic immersion." This is the dedicated presence of the therapist with the client, or the friend with the friend, unhampered by judgment, plans to fix or change him or her, or personal projections.

Mindful presence means that one person enters the interior garden of the other and walks through it without trampling any of the flowers, without blaming anyone for the presence of weeds, with great appreciation for all the time, pain, and growth it took to be the way it is. How can this be accomplished in our relationships? It takes an engaged focus that happens best in contemplation, the mindfully bare attention of an alert and caring witness. A contemplative presence involves listening, seeing, and attending without the diversionary mind-sets of fear, desire, control, judgment, or projection.

Enlightenment thus leads to lightening ourselves of the heavy wardrobe of ego. Then we automatically let the light through, since our ego is no longer in the way. We become a vehicle for the light, not a roadblock to it. To stay with ourself or our friend or partner in this way requires that we be free of the need to clear things up or assume control. One person simply accepts the other's truth no matter how unclear, broken, desperate, or fragmented it may be. In mindful and compassionate presence, it becomes quite acceptable for us or others to be adrift rather than on course, to miss the target, to feel longing without fulfillment. Every variety of human experience is granted hospitality in this zendo of loving-kindness. In the Buddhist tradition, Avalokiteshvara is the buddha of compassion, whose name literally means "he who hears the cries of those in pain." To hear must be a healing practice.

Empathic presence means listening to someone's pain with what I call the five A's: attention, acceptance, appreciation, affection, and allowing. We pay attention without being distracted. We accept what is said without editing, adding, or blanking. We feel a genuine caring about what happened and what might happen to this person. We allow whatever feelings or silences or head trips the other employs in this moment without attempting to blame him, stop him, or criticize him. The same five A's are the defining features of support, mirroring, caring, and intimate love.

A friend who is suffering in our presence soon knows with certainty that it is always all right to be in disarray, depressed, or confused when around us. He knows he will not be expected to "snap out of it." He knows he will not be talked out of it with comforting quotations from Buddha or Christ. The person in pain is granted access to the hard and pained corners in her psyche within this holding environment of empathy. She has found a companion who can sit with her in the dark. Her worst side can become visible without her being blamed or shamed.

This spiritual practice of nonjudgmental presence has paradoxical implications. For when a feeling state or an immediate experience is granted a hearing in full safety, something wonderfully opening happens. A shift occurs automatically. Once someone experiences a self-validating moment to the full, an inner permission to let go and move on is granted from deep in the psyche. Bearings are gained when the pilot has an honest view of where the ship is, no matter how lost or off course. The poet Christopher Buckley recommends that we "open to something on its own terms." This practice of empathy is nothing less than the unconditional yes applied to the immediate experience of pain.

Feeling sorry for someone is not compassion, since it is ultimately hierarchical. Compassion happens when we accept the other as an equal and the other's pain as what we may feel sometime too. "Let's just sit beside one another and look at this together. This happened to you. Let me be here with you as we witness this together." I am not the witness of her reality; we are the witnesses of it. This is a crucial feature of the paradox. The other also has to step back and look at her own experience as a compassionate and alert witness, not as a judge, victim, or prosecutor. Only in mutual mindfulness can the healing shift occur.

How does the shift occur? When we contemplate together mindfully, we see the other person with more empathy and he sees himself with more empathy. Such a softening toward the event and oneself in it makes for a reframing of the story. If it was shame based, it must have been seen with censure. A mindful contemplation dissolves that. If it was fear based, it can now be opened to alternatives, and that makes for a less trapped feeling, on which fear thrives.

In this application of empathic mindfulness I gain because I learn how to see with *loving curiosity*. I can allow for the given of a lunar landscape rather than demand a lush garden. I am present to what is, not rejecting it in favor of my own preferred version or trying to "get this over with." I have no questions or suggestions, only simple attention to the words, feelings, mood, gestures, body language, eyes, and any other sources of communication. I am present fully because I have a beginner's mind. I mirror back the feelings of the other. I am clear about what I feel without interfering with the feelings of the other. When I combine mirroring and congruence in this way, I am imparting to the other the equivalent of physical holding. I am providing a container in which even the most terrifying moments of the other can be validated, endured, and survived.

Our mental overlays such as fear, the desire to control or fix, judgment or censure, and illusion or projection are normal for all of us hearing any story. We automatically think of solutions when we are presented with problems. Mindfulness means disembarking from that train of thought. In the style of mindfulness, our mind-sets can be suspended so we can become really present to someone's naked anguish. If I notice myself judging, I simply witness it and come back to the moment and to what the person facing me is experiencing. If I notice that I am transferring my own fears onto the other, I tap myself on the shoulder, metaphorically, and redirect my attention to what the other is feeling.

I notice that when my mind-sets (fear, judgment, blame, need to fix, attachment to an outcome) recede, I am much more in touch with my heart and its empathy. I respond with an understanding that does not configure the other as a victim. I see it all simply and only as *fact,* and the fact speaks for itself and appears before me with a powerful and challenging poignancy.

Our empathy extends to ourselves too. We all construct a life narrative to condemn or exculpate ourselves or others. From this story that we keep telling ourselves and others, we form a set of governing scripts; for example, we are helpless victims of our past or of how people are treating us now. These scripts explain our condition in life and get us off the hook about amending our lives in conscientious ways. Mindful presence in our own pain is a release from that sheltering illusion. It is coming into the explicitly real rather than hiding in the implicitly illusory.

WHEN CHEER DOESN'T WORK

I often notice the temptation to make cheering remarks when a friend is depressed or in anguish about something that has happened. The tried and true platitudes of hope and promise, however, interrupt what is happening in the moment for this desperate person. Sometimes all someone can feel is despair. In the dark night of the soul, we lose track of the library of wisdom with all its reassuring words about how things will get better, there is always a brighter side, death leads to resurrection. The archetypal value of spiritual truths is not always available to consciousness when we are in the depths of despair. That void deserves its own time and space.

Hope is a clarion that can only be sounded—or hearkened to—when the time is right. We are mindful when we honor what is personally true in this moment, not what is universally true for all time. This articulation of our truth, albeit limited, takes precedence over what we believe to be true in the overall scheme of things.

An existential reality is conditioned by its moment and our mood. This is the figure, what we experience conditionally. The essential archetypal reality is the ground, unconditioned. The existential reality faces us right now; the essential reality is not visible until we shift into it. The challenge is to stay steadfastly with the here-and-now existential reality, however unsavory, while the essential truth—always comforting—hovers in the wings awaiting the audience that will happen in its own time.

The paradox is that going further into despair is what grants access to hope, going fully into pain grants access to healing, going fully into the dark opens to the light. An unconditionally embraced predicament becomes a threshold to what comes next. The "either . . . or" changes to "both . . . and." How? We no longer jump into the unexplored territory of any mood or pain with the banner of hope and declare it under our control. We simply stay put in our own and the other's truth, and that fidelity creates the milieu in which transformation may come about. This is quite understandable in a psyche like ours in which opposites continually constellate like stars in patterns that both please and predict.

THE FERTILE VOID

When we find out that the great Void is full of ch'i, we know there is no such thing as nothingness.

—CHANG TSAI

The Roman poet Ovid wrote: "Do you not see that the year has four parts in imitation of our own lifetime?" The seasons of nature reflect the periods of light and dark in our own lives. To expect permanent springtime is not an adult—or natural—way of living in time. The year begins with spring, in which new life appears both in plants and in animals. In summer this life is in full bloom as young animals are born or are growing and fruits are ripening. In the fall abundant growth is ready for harvesting. In winter all goes into a restful and nonproducing state as many animals hibernate. In the following spring all comes back to life as the cycle recommences. Pain and ending characterize each phase and so do joy and renewal.

Likewise in our lives, we experience the four seasons: newness, fullness, harvesting, and repose, and then it all begins again. Each ushers in its own painful challenge. Dark seasons are prerequisite to renewal. A rose can only ensure its reappearance in the following spring if it lets itself go to seed and die. The seeds are ready only at the end of its life of blossoming, and only such seasoned seeds will be capable of sprouting in the future. The end is the necessary assurance for resurrection. We may have to die in many ways in order to live in new ways. Nature is a model of mindful letting go, since she does not feel pain in parting as we do. She simply observes her seasons and passes through them, however dark, without debate. Our purpose is not to be like Nature in that way, however. We imitate her letting go but not her apparent stoicism. Our tears are precious, necessary, and part of what make us such endearing creatures.

Our planet has vast areas of desert in its topography. Archetypally, these represent the dark side of the blooming world. Nature is a metaphor of our inner life. Thus in our psyches we can expect a tormenting desertlike time in which nothing seems to be moving or growing in us. Such a torturous void is the unlit era in life when exuberance is gone, when nothing seems to succeed in reviving or renewing us, when things do not improve no matter how much effort we expend, when our spiritual practices become flat and uncomforting. This is the ruthless shadow side of our psychic world, a wilderness with no visible horizon of relief.

We appreciate deserts as useful topographies of the planet. But we do not often trust that our own empty and desolate moments can be incubation periods in the evolutionary ecology of our inner world. Each day includes a noon of clarity and a midnight of mystery. Since this happens so regularly and for all of us, it must be legitimate and even useful to be fully clear and happy at times and at other times to be unhappy and in the dark. Indeed, in the dark, bread rises. We are nourished by light *and* dark. The spiritual style is to find a way to say yes mindfully to both.

Distressing voids are thus challenges to stay with ourselves. To stay is to say yes. Mindfulness is a practice of attending and staying. Mindful presence in the void happens when we pay attention to what is with no attempt to understand it and when we stay in it with no attempt to end it. If we simply stay with the experience of the void, something eventually opens in it and us.

What is born from our yes to the void is not emptiness but spaciousness, transparency—two bright descriptions of the very no-self we find in spiritual awakening. We say yes to the silent dark and it reveals itself as a necessary—even kindly—oasis in our inner landscape. We no longer seek things or people to rescue us. Eventually the space becomes as significant and as supportive as the things or persons who were supposed to fill it.

In the void we feel fragmented and even unreal. British psychiatrist D. W. Winnicott says: "It is unhealthy to deny the innate capacity of every human being to become unintegrated, depersonalized, and to feel that the world is unreal." In other words, it is a given of life that at times we will feel isolated and unreal. We will feel lost and bewildered. Thoreau's life presents a natural metaphor. He considered wandering aimlessly in the woods as a spiritual practice: "Not till we are lost . . . do we begin to find ourselves and realize where we are and the infinite extent of our relations."

We do fall apart. That is a given. Our mindful yes is how we live through it. The proper etiquette in the void is not getting back in control but simply sitting in the dark. This takes trust and humility. Trust means believing that this would not be happening if it were not meant to help us grow. Humility means accepting reality with no attempt to outsmart it.

In ancient Egypt the scarab (or dung beetle) was a sacred symbol of unity and self-regeneration. The scarab's evolution from egg to adult is a metaphor of our journey to spiritual maturity. The scarab lays and fertilizes its eggs in dung, the most abject form of matter, thus tying its metamorphosis to the earth with a gritty matter-of-factness. The scarab rolls the dung containing its eggs into a ball, pushes it along by day, and buries it in the sand at night. The twelve-hour cycle of moving from the light, the known, to the dark, the unconscious, represents the necessary roles of both consciousness and unconsciousness—clarity and void—in the generation and gestation of spiritual adulthood.

Growth requires a journey embracing both light and dark. The beetle pushes its ball of dung over the earth, attending to it, staying with it, loyal to it, and trusting the alchemical process of transformation that is occurring. This is the combination of trust and humility.

The egg of the beetle comes into form as a larva. That larva then feeds on the dung, the base earth itself, in order to develop. The larva of the scarab next becomes a gooey, undifferentiated cocoon. This dark night of the soul, the void, in which we are no one in particular, feeling unreal, is now signified as also necessary for our evolution into spiritual maturity. When the scarab emerges from the cocoon, it is fully grown and ready to continue the cycle and generate its own off-spring. The seasons of the scarab's life are the seasons of our spiritual life: birth, death, rebirth.

The metaphor of the scarab shows the rational mind that cycles are not mechanical. They are daily and often risky opportunities for re-birth. In nature there is a light that arises from the dark. That is dawn. There is a birth that arises from death. That is vegetation. There is a renewal that emerges from endings. That is spring. We carry those same promises in our heart, and all it takes for them to keep occurring is a yes to life with all its compulsory foldings and all its certain unfoldings. We become spiritually mature when we go willingly into the dark and impart to the world the light that results, when we say yes to endings and notice new beginnings, when we say yes to losses and discover renewals. How does this happen? It is the built-in result of our unconditional yes.

Finally, Shakespeare also expresses how the seasons of nature and our connection to them teach us who we are and where our chal-lenges lie. In the Duke's speech in *As You Like It* he personifies nature's dark possibilities as wise guides that assist us in finding our-selves with mindfulness and feeling:

> Are not these woods
> More free from peril than the envious court?
> Here feel we but the penalty of Adam,
> The seasons' difference, as the icy fang

And churlish chiding of the winter's wind,
Which, when it bites and blows upon my body,
Even till I shrink with cold, I smile and say
"This is no flattery: *these are counselors*
That feelingly persuade me what I am." (author's
emphasis)

As I say yes to the fact of suffering, may I accept the dark side of life and find a way through it, and may I then become an escort of compassion to those who also suffer.

FIVE

PEOPLE ARE NOT LOVING
AND LOYAL ALL THE TIME

For we must be clear that to live or love only where one can trust, where there is security and containment, where one cannot be hurt or let down, where what is pledged in words is forever binding, means really to be out of harm's way and so to be out of real life. And it does not matter what is this vessel of trust—analysis, marriage, church, or law, any human relationship.

—JAMES HILLMAN

SOME PEOPLE act dishonestly; some lie; some are hypocritical. Part of growing up psychologically and spiritually is noticing all this but without censure or retaliation. We do not willingly allow others to be dishonest or hurtful toward us if we can prevent it. If they are, we ask for amends. If all we do fails, we let go. If those we respect as teachers or models turn out to be hypocrites in their personal lives, that does not diminish the legitimacy of their teaching. An adult knows that the teachings are the teacher. The person who teaches is only a mouthpiece, and a piece is hardly ever perfect. I appreciate the ferry ride even when the ferryman proves to be a rascal.

Sometimes people keep their promises and sometimes they do not.

Sometimes people love us loyally and faithfully, even unconditionally. Sometimes they hate, reject, abandon, or betray us. An adult has learned to take all this in stride. We feel the pain, but it does not devastate or destabilize us. We receive love with openness and appreciation. We receive loyalty with gratitude. We handle betrayal with the strength we gained from our psychological work. We let go of retaliation and act with compassion thanks to our spiritual practices. We do not want to be so strongly affected by what others do that we lose our own ability to love, which is all that matters to us now.

Some people will like us and some dislike us; some come through for us and some betray us; some care tenderly about our feelings and some trample them underfoot. Accepting this variety as a given makes it less likely that we will let the reactions of others determine our personal worth. Our spiritual practice is a straightforward yes to the full spectrum of human responses we will encounter in our lifetime. This delivers us from having to feel bad about ourselves or to make others wrong for not loving us. No human being was ever loved or treated respectfully by everyone. That has to settle in as a simple fact of life. Then we mindfully notice others' reactions to us and go on loving and respecting others no matter what. Our capacity to love survives unscathed.

Our spiritual practice of loving-kindness toward all beings helps us join this tougher skin to a tender heart. This is how hurts help us find our own potential for unconditional love and unconditional compassion. People do things that injure us, but later we realize that was how they pushed us through a gate in ourselves that we never guessed was there. The hurt we felt was the sensation of being pushed.

We may distinguish two kinds of hurt: intentional and consequent. For example, a given of entering a relationship is that either partner can end it. Intentional hurt happens when people leave us in a cruel and thoughtless way. This leads us to feel sorrow, and in spiritual consciousness, we feel this pain without a plan to retaliate. Consequent hurt happens as the natural and inevitable result of events and reasonable choices. For example, our partner ends our relationship in a kind and respectful way. We both tried our best but the relationship was not meant to be. We feel hurt, but this is consequent hurt, not intentional hurt, and it leads to grief and moving on.

Sometimes we hurt others. If we do so intentionally, we experience guilt, the built-in signal that helps us know it is time to make amends. If hurt happens as a result of a legitimate choice, such as leaving an unhealthy relationship, we do not blame ourselves. We find ways to leave with kindliness, not acrimony, and we remain available to share in our partner's grieving for however long that may be appropriate.

When others do not acknowledge us or they snub, reject, or ignore us, it is perfectly natural to feel hurt, since we are made of penetrable stuff. Our work as healthy psychological adults is to feel the hurt rather than run from it. Our practice as spiritually mature beings is to feel the hurt without having to retaliate. If we feel the hurt more intensely than seems to fit the bill, we may want to examine ourselves and ask if our ego has reared its entitled and demanding head. If it has, we can look at our FACE in the mirror and say:

Fear: I am afraid that I will not survive if everyone does not love me, and this is how I am a source of suffering to myself.

Attachment: I am attached to a very specific version of what I am owed, and this is how I am a source of suffering to myself.

Control: I need to control others' reactions to me, and this is how I am a source of suffering to myself.

Entitlement: I believe I am entitled to love and loyalty from everyone, and insist on it, and this is how I am a source of suffering to myself.

I am letting go of fear by showing more love and finding excitement in life's challenges.

I am letting go of attachment to my version of how others should act and I accept the given of life that not everyone will be loving, truthful, honest, caring, or loyal to me all the time.

I am letting go of control and let others love or dislike me as they choose.

I am letting go of my insistence that I be loved and respected by everyone, and I choose to focus instead on being loving and respectful toward everyone I meet. This is what matters to me now.

I am always aware that I also am not loving and loyal all the time and
  I am working on that.

THE LIFELONG INFLUENCE
OF CHILDHOOD

I tried to hide my first lip hairs. I even recall a sense of shame about
them. It seemed dangerous to become fully grown-up in my close-
knit Italian family. I thought I might lose my place in the household
if I looked like I was getting ready to leave. My need for belonging
was much stronger than my impulse to grow. The price of belonging
is sometimes to stay small.

A sense of belonging happens in a holding environment, a secure
space that contains and welcomes all that we are and fosters our
unique directions of growth. Other mammals run some*where* when
they are in crisis or threatened, but primates run to some*one*. To secure that family connection, we might have had to give up our adult
needs, including our growth needs. For instance, we might have had
to edit ourselves rather than engage in free speech. Some televised
movies begin with the statement "This film has been modified to fit
your screen." This might also apply to us. Our true self might have
been modified to fit our family screen. We may then have created
necessary fictions, such as a suspicion that new hairs are dangerous
and have to be hidden. After all, a sanctuary, no matter how drafty,
is preferable to an empty house.

When we are young, we reach out for understanding. We become
angry if we don't get it. When our parents don't respond to our need
for understanding, we feel despair. Sometimes nothing we do works
to get us the love we want, and the household itself—meant to be a
sanctuary—becomes scary and dangerous. We feel panic—fright
without the possibility of solution. It is even more injurious to us when
the parent to whom we would run is the one who terrifies us. Rather
than a nurturant mother, we may have had a witch mother, and there
was no refuge in which to feel safe. With such betrayal we might become emotionally unable to relate effectively. For instance, we may

continually distrust others, especially intimate partners. Using our two-handed practice (see page 7) we can hold both "People can't always be trusted" and "I do not shut down because of this fact."

As we notice the disturbing given that anyone can betray us, we accept the consequent fact that our trust in others has to be provisional rather than unreserved. The role of witness confers strength upon us, the power to appreciate reliability but no longer to need it to be absolute. We now trust ourselves both to receive loyalty gratefully and to handle betrayal firmly while never vengefully.

Trust begins in the earliest moments of life. Some of us had reliable parents, some not so reliable. We may now seek adult partners who reverse or repeat our original experience. It is a powerful given of life that childhood maintains a long-term influence over our choices both individually and in relationship.

Our desires and fears from the past are indelibly recorded in the very cells of our bodies. We keep looking for the love we missed. We keep fearing a repetition of the blows we cannot forget. We keep seeking one or all of the five A's that represent our childhood and adult intimacy needs: attention, acceptance, appreciation, affection, allowing.

Some of us were given too little. Some of us were given too much. Parents who overprized us were instilling needs rather than fulfilling them. Needs unfulfilled and underfulfilled become exaggerated later. Needs overfulfilled may lead to engulfment fears, a sense that intimacy is intrusive no matter how tender. Needs underfulfilled may lead to an insatiability. Needs fulfilled stably and consistently can be satisfied by adult partners later in life with a moderate amount of the five A's, the only amount an adult needs and the only amount another adult can or will give.

Some of us do not recall what happened in childhood. We do not quite recall how we were treated till a partner treats us the same way our parents did, then: "This has happened before." The more we can remember, the more likely we are to grieve the past and let go of it so we can meet other adults not as figures from our past but as real people in the present. This is the journey to mindfulness. If our relationships open old wounds, if we find ourselves in a forest of emotional pain, we realize that we are there on horseback. Something is already and always present to carry us through. The horse is our innate gift for facing our issues and dealing with them, our mindful awareness, our attitude of yes. This horse knows the trail through and out. Riding this horse of mindfulness, we are able to move on, the adult option when we cannot get what we need where we are. A Zen saying helps us: "This being the case, how shall I proceed?" That is so much more an adult question than "This being the case, who is at fault or why is this happening to me?"

Parents who have an understanding of themselves and have resolved their own childhood issues create an atmosphere in which safe attachment, and thereby optimal growth, can occur. What matters to parents and to children is not what happened to them or between them but whether what happened was addressed, processed, and resolved. Resolution leads to health; disorganized experience leads to fragmentation. Mental health is not about what happened but about how we manage what happened.

TAKING CARE OF YOURSELF AS YOU OPEN TO OTHERS

It is a given of relationships that the five A's may not consistently come our way and certainly not to the extent we would wish. An unconditional yes to this fact about our partner upgrades us from a fairy-tale mentality to adult realization. As we kindly accept the reality of others' inadequacy, our own needs begin to change. We no longer need what cannot be had: "I let go of wanting what isn't here now." We align our needs with the available resources in our partner. Paradoxically, as we reduce our unrealistic expectations, our partner feels less pressured and actually stretches so that more need fulfillment comes our way after all—sometimes the acceptance of reality can help reality to change.

Our adult challenge is to become self-nurturant while at the same time able to give and receive the five A's. What does it mean to be self-nurturant? It is to find some of what you need within yourself. How do you build inner resources so you can do this? "Find it in yourself" means finding it in the part of you that is committed to engaging in spiritual practices, not in the needy part of you that comes to the fore during a crisis or in desperation. You can learn to trust that there is a sane, wise, and nurturant resource within you. In fact, the more you know what you really want, the less desperately you need it. This happens because your self-esteem, confidence, and clarity grow. Here are some helpful practices:

• Sit mindfully in your present reality for fifteen minutes each day. This means holding your predicament without blame of yourself or others, with no attempt to change, fix, or end it, and with no attachment or repulsion. Simply be with what is going on, be as with it if you were holding your experience lovingly in your lap, like the Madonna of the *Pietà* by Michelangelo.

• Notice where your deepest needs, values, and wishes are and follow them with an engaged focus. In other words, find what you love and get into it no matter how awkward it feels to do so. We find our deepest needs, values, and wishes when we grant ourselves the five A's: We pay attention to what we feel and what makes us grow; we accept ourselves as we are all the way to the bottom; we appreciate, feel affection for, and value ourselves; we allow ourselves to try new things. All this happens as a result of an unconditional yes to ourselves.

• Remind yourself of your place in the universe. Consciously recall your family of origin, your ancestors, and then your connection to all humanity. Do this both for a sense of continuity and to ask your ancestors' support in your finding a rich heritage of strength within yourself.

• Begin to configure other people as fellow pilgrims not as shrines meant to give you comfort or answers. The shrine is in your own heart. Other people can relate to you helpfully but not complete you.

• Act with kindness and respect toward all beings. Do this as a spiritual practice, not as a tactic to manipulate others.

- Make contact with nature in different ways each day. Commune with it silently and in dialogue. Nature is the mother of a sense of belonging, and that *is* a sense of self.
- Give up the standard escape hatches of alcohol and drugs. Examine your lifestyle to see what escape hatches you rely on and give up the unhealthy ones. If you suffer from addiction, turn for help to a twelve-step program.
- Work on yourself through psychotherapy or counseling. Recommit yourself to your spiritual practice and join groups or read books that support it.

At the same time, it is not infantile to seek moments of being held and of being taken care of by other adults. Indeed, such moments are important to our happiness, and in any case, given the fact of change and impermanence built into us, all we can ask of one another are moments. These moments of love from other adults are precious and healing. They are the unconditional yes to our existence and to our lovability. In such a moment we might say: "When you hold me this way, I feel you are fulfilling needs I gave up on long ago." Being loved helps us not give up on ourselves.

Nature and spirituality tell us we are all interconnected, but traditional Western psychology says that our life task is to separate and individuate. That can feel like a split between our natural instinct and our psychological work. We benefit best from a view that accommodates the full range of our humanity. The central realization of mature spiritual consciousness about interconnectedness means that as humans in a world of others, our needs are interactive. We do not develop character by discharging the tension of our own drives but by committing ourselves to continual bonding in love with others no matter what happens or how they behave. Connectedness is as unconditional as love, since it survives under any conditions.

In the connections that fulfill us we discover how utterly open our hearts can be; in those that disappoint us we find out how tenderly vulnerable our hearts can become. In any case, it is ultimately between one heart and another that the manna of human wholeness is exchanged, bestowed, and blessed. How fortunate we humans are that love, just love, turns out to be the only dawn it takes to dispel our isolation.

> *When I love thee not, chaos is come again.*
> — WILLIAM SHAKESPEARE, *Othello*

GIVENS OF ADULT RELATING

In a previous book, *How to Be an Adult in Relationships,* I explored the hallmarks of mature, lasting love. When we accept the fact that people are not loving or loyal all the time, we take a major step toward becoming an adult in our relationships. But there are other important givens of adult relationships that also call for the yes of aligning surrender. Use this list as a personal checklist to see how comfortable you are with these givens. To which ones do you easily say yes and which do you argue with?

• You may not be treated with all the fuss you received in childhood, and this may feel like the equivalent of not being loved. It is normal that the level of attention paid to you changes throughout life from rapt attention in infancy to quasi invisibility in old age.

• No matter how your parents may have mistreated you, they are not stopping you now from doing at least some of the therapeutic work it takes to recover. You will always see how your parents influenced the shape your life has taken, but you can let go of blaming them.

• When the gnawing question is "Why am I not getting what I want in life?" one of the questions behind it may be "What am I still carrying with me from the past?"

• Love is a teaching device. When your parents showed you one or more of the five A's, they were doing more than just fulfilling your needs. They were teaching you exactly how to give the five A's to yourself and others. Every cell of your body remembers how.

• Your mind may be saying, "I want a peaceful relationship," but your body may want what it had in childhood: the drama of recurrent fear and unsatisfied desire. A giveaway of this dynamic is if you have a tendency to "stir the pot," getting back at a partner rather than addressing, processing, and resolving the issue you are both facing. Seeking drama in relationships means fearing and desiring uproar at the same time. For instance, in real conflict resolution, you stop arguing when you notice it is not working. If you continue to argue, you're looking for drama more than harmony.

• The purpose of relationships is the same as the purpose of our work and life: to become fully evolved adults who give and receive the five A's abundantly: attention, acceptance, appreciation, affection, and allowing. Anything less leads to a stunting of ourselves.

• The criterion for being in a relationship is the same as that of any important choice in life: Is this a context in which I will find the safety to be myself; to live in accord with my deepest needs, values, wishes, and potentials; and to fulfill my life purposes?

• An ego-based question in a relationship is "What can I get out of this?" A spiritually healthy question might be "What will it take to be a contributor here?"

• In a committed relationship or friendship, partners can challenge one another without fear of disrupting or ending the connection.

• Some people, especially introverts, find strength by withdrawing into themselves. Can you handle that as a partner's style, or will you take it as rejection?

• Sex is so layered with needs, history, and ego that its meaning is often secret even from you.

• In a relationship, you always face two possibilities: reality and fantasy. "How much of this relationship is based on fact and how much on my own fictional sense of or wishful thinking about what is going on or who this person is?"

• In an uneasy relationship, an adult moves away from "He's to blame" to "I am choosing to be here."

• You may seek—or be in—an attachment that *feels* good, and call it love, rather than a connection that *is* good, which is love.

• The central fear of intimacy is that you will have to give up control over how someone loves you. If a partner gets too close, you may feel the fear of engulfment. If a partner goes too far away, you may feel the fear of abandonment. You may be fearful in some way all your life, but you no longer have to be fear based. There are ways of working with fear in therapy and in spiritual practice.

• If you are sensitive to abandonment, it is natural to become terrified when you are criticized or when someone shows disappointment in you. This may be because it feels like a serious or permanent rejection, a severing of a desperately needed bond: "This criticism means she doesn't like me, wants to leave me, and won't love me anymore. When people don't like me, it is my fault."

• The fact that "love is blind" gives us all a chance to be loved by somebody.

• The choice in communication is between two approaches: adult problem solving with focus on the issue or an ego-competitive or defensive style with focus on winning, self-assertion, and not losing face.

• Can you distinguish between needs and beliefs that you have a need? For instance, as an adult you do not need someone to take care of you, but you may believe that you do.

• A soul mate is not the one who says he or she is your other half but the one who shows you that you are whole.

• "He is all I have": This may be why you are staying in an untenable relationship. Such resignation to pain leads to despair, a loss of your lively energy. Despair in this context is believing there is no chance for the five A's. That is a reason to mourn rather than to give up.

• Expectation is a personal longing that we try to get someone else to take care of. An adult has given that up.

• When you find a partner's traits distressing, it is important not to attempt to change her or him but to work on how to handle what you find unappealing. It is harder to defang the bobcat than to learn ways to protect ourselves.

• No person or event can force a negative reaction from you when you are committed to standards of loving-kindness.

• We imperfect human beings need each other, not perfection, to become happy and whole. We are "good enough" for each other as we are.

• There is a central difference between living in a committed relationship and in single life. In single life the virtues of humility, compassion, attentiveness, caring, and patience are recommended. In a relationship they are required.

A CHECKLIST ON BOUNDARIES IN OUR RELATIONSHIPS

No one has the whole set of keys to the inner chambers of your being, and no one should. There always remains the mystery of your core and the task of maintaining boundaries neither too loosely nor too rigidly. We know our own preferences and moods rather than living reactively to those of others. As adults our love is unconditional, but our commitment is conditioned by how cooperative our partner is and how reasonable the demands of the relationship are. Here is a list that may help us see where we stand. The left side is about relationship as accommodation. The right side is about relationship as negotiation.

When you give up your boundaries in a relationship you	*When your boundaries are intact in a relationship you*
• Break commitments with friends because the person so important to you is suddenly available	• Design your schedule in a cooperative way but respectful of your own needs and plans
• Do not notice how unhappy you are, since enduring is your main concern	• Recognize when you are happy or unhappy
• Do more and more for less and less	• Do more when to do more gets results (your commitment to help fits and is based on its effectiveness)
• Require the approval of others in order to have self-esteem	• Take others' criticism as information with no diminishment of self-esteem

- Live hopefully while continuing to wait for change

- Are satisfied as long as you are coping and surviving

- Let another's promises or minimal improvement maintain your stalemate

- Have few hobbies because you have no attention span for self-directed activity; you are other directed

- Make exceptions for this person for things you would not tolerate in anyone else and accept his or her alibis or lies

- Are manipulated by flattery so that you lose objectivity

- Keep trying to create intimacy with a narcissist

- Are so strongly affected by another that you have become obsessive about him

- Will forsake every personal limit to get sex or the promise of it

- See your partner as causing your excitement

- Feel hurt and victimized but dare not show anger

- Live optimistically because you are co-working on change

- Are only satisfied if you are thriving

- Are encouraged only by mutual commitment to change

- Have excited interest in self-enhancing hobbies and projects whether or not the other joins you in them

- Have a personal standard that, albeit flexible, applies to everyone and are not afraid to ask for accountability

- Appreciate feedback and can distinguish it from attempts to manipulate

- Are open to relationships only with partners with whom reciprocal love is possible

- Are appropriately affected by your partner's behavior and take it as information

- Integrate sex so that you can enjoy it but never at the cost of your own integrity

- See your partner as stimulating your excitement

- Let yourself feel anger, say "Ouch!" and embark on a program to change your situation for the better

- Act out of compliance, compromise, and appeasement

- Do favors that you inwardly resist while being motivated by obligation or indebtedness (cannot say no)

- Cannot dismiss lingering guilt even after reasonable amends or no fault at all

- Disregard your own intuition in favor of wishful thinking

- Allow your partner to abuse you or your children, family, or friends

- Mostly feel afraid and confused

- Are enmeshed more and more in a drama that unfolds beyond your control

- Are living a life that is not yours and are perhaps not quite aware of it

- Believe you have no right to privacy or a life of your own

- Never believe you have given enough

- Fear your partner will leave or punish you if you disappoint him or her and cannot imagine or tolerate life without your partner

- Act out of agreement and negotiation

- Only do favors that are motivated by choice, and you cannot be guilt-tripped (can say no)

- Are satisfied and no longer resentful once amends are made

- Honor intuitions and distinguish them from wishes

- Insist others' boundaries be as safeguarded as your own

- Mostly feel secure and clear

- Are always aware of choices rather than feeling trapped or at the mercy of the other

- Are living a life that mostly reflects your deepest needs, values, and wishes

- Protect and enjoy your private matters without having to lie or be surreptitious

- Give generously and reasonably and then let go

- Trust yourself to be able to handle comings and goings and to survive quite comfortably if left alone

- Arrange things so that your partner will be protected from your real feelings or truth

- Tolerate your partner's addiction(s) even when they lead to abuse

- Forsake your own moral standards to please or hold on to someone

- Place your physical health at risk

- Are swayed by looks, charm, rhetoric, sex, history together, or financial security

- Give, loan, or invest money inappropriately

- Lose objectivity, intelligence, and personal powers

The above entries define
CODEPENDENCY.

- Cannot be blackmailed by threats of abandonment

- Assertively and kindly express to the other what you feel, think, and want

- Confront addictive behavior and detach if change is not forthcoming

- Maintain your own principles with consistency

- Protect your body in all circumstances

- Enjoy the extras as desserts but are never controlled by them

- Handle money matters wisely, generously, and objectively

- Maintain your full range of personal discernment and power

The above entries define
SELF-PARENTING.

EGOLESS LOVE

Being reconciled to the love others can give means the end of putting demands on them. We cherish love unconditionally, in any form or size. At the same time, we do not make a commitment to someone if the love that person offers is inadequate. We do appreciate it when we have been given the best this person has to offer. But if the best is still unsatisfactory, the only question is: What do I do next? Most of us ask instead: What should he do next to satisfy me? In the face of what *is*, why do we come up with a *should*?

Unconditional love happens best within a context of plenitude rather than neediness. Such inner fullness overflows spontaneously into the five A's, which is a technology for openness. When I am present in those five unconditional ways, I find myself opening. And when I give the five A's to myself, I grow in self-esteem.

Our spiritual practices have a direct impact on the possibility of our showing love in relationships in an adult way: Mindfulness helps us practice attention, acceptance, and allowing. Loving-kindness helps us show affection and appreciation.

As a spiritual practice, ask yourself about the signs that your love for someone is truly unconditional:

• You feel a sense of connectedness with the other that endures and cannot be supplanted no matter what.

• You consistently have well-meaning thoughts and are wishing the best for the other.

• You act kindly, at times even anonymously, with no expectation of anything in return.

• You sense your heart opening when you are with the other or thinking of her or him.

• You maintain a commitment to nurture the other and the relationship more than your own ego demands.

• You are no longer pushed or arrested by fears of closeness to or distance from the other.

• You do not engage in ego competitiveness or aggression, actively or passively.

• You are sensitive to how the other feels and go to any length not to hurt him or her intentionally.

• You have an effortlessly compassionate, forgiving, generous, and nonretaliatory attitude in your thoughts and actions. (There is no vindictive force in the universe. Revenge is exclusive to humanity.)

• You keep your own boundaries intact so that your love is always unconditional, but your commitment is intelligently and appropriately conditional.

- You are aware of your partner's negative traits and you see them with compassion and amusement without letting them impinge upon you. Am I willing to play on relationship's full checkerboard of light and dark?

- Finally, unconditional love is entirely in the present tense. You do not hold a grudge from the past or hold the other's past against her or him. As Don Murray said to Marilyn Monroe in *Bus Stop* when she offered to tell him of her profligate past: "I like you the way you are. What do I care how you got that way?"

As I say yes to the givens of relating, may I find love and abundance in myself and others, and may I always remain loving to others no matter how disloyal they are to me.

SIX

REFUGES FROM THE GIVENS

W E L I V E in a society that fights the givens tooth and nail. The accent on youth and beauty as well as on wealth and prestige leads to suffering in those who do not fit the bill. This society says no to life's implacable conditions and works hard on inventing products and procedures that can reverse them. As long as that is the case, we are not in a world grounded in the truth of things; rather, we are afraid of life's inevitable vicissitudes. An example is aging. As we become older, more battle scarred by relationships, less appealing, we become invisible or inconvenient. This is why it is so important to have a set of values that cherishes not that which is superficial but that which represents the enduring values of virtue and integrity. Then as we age we have everything left.

RELIGION AS A REFUGE

Fear will never be a secular phenomenon. It is deeply associated with the idea that there are powers beyond us that can harm or help us. This is why religion has so much to say about letting go of fear, and also why it does so much to scare us. Our deepest fears surround the conditions of our mortal existence. Religion attempts to respond to that scared place within us. For example, there are a number of Christian responses to the givens. To the given of impermanence, Saint Paul says: "When this earthly tent is folded up, there awaits us a tabernacle not made by hands." Earthly things are impermanent, but we are promised a heavenly home that is eternal. And in the Christian tradition, the fact that things do not always go according to plan is offset by the divine plan and a reliable providence that can be trusted to make things work out for the best.

In the face of a lack of fairness, most religions declare that there will be a final judgment day at which the good will be rewarded and the evil punished. To the universal fact of suffering Jesus says: "Take up your cross and follow me. . . . You shall have a reward in heaven." Suffering has a redemptive and salvific value in Christianity and in most religion traditions. To the fact that people are not loyal or loving all the time we have the consolation of knowing that "God is love." Though humans may desert us, God never fails us. Finally, we hear that none of life's givens will be more than we can bear, as Saint Paul states the promise of Christ: "My grace is sufficient for thee."

Every religion states that our mortal world is not all there is. Its givens are not the last word. Religions validate the fact of grace and help us in proclaiming the unconditional yes. In this way religious resources are positive. They become negative when they are used as a shield or escape from having to feel the full impact of the conditions of existence. Then religion buffers and minimizes the importance of this life, offering a repeal of the givens in a life to come. When life here on earth is only seen as a passage to the real life in paradise, the refuges of religion become merely escape hatches.

A mature religious consciousness offers skillful means to face up to life's givens boldly and even cheerfully. Mature religion honors this life here and now as an exciting evolutionary challenge, as enormously significant, and as the right place and time for the fulfillment of our destiny precisely *through* the givens. Jesus is then a model of the unconditional yes, as Saint Paul says: "In him there was only Yes."

Faith is real when it hails life's terms with no entitlement to an exemption and no guarantees they will be reversed beyond the grave. The God who annuls the givens for us is the God of no to the life he created. That God is a rescuer of victims and a punisher of offenders. The God who joins us in the givens, as Jesus and the saints did, is the higher power of yes. That God is the comrade of humans.

The traditional view that God will intervene, deus ex machina, to abrogate or minimize the givens is not an adult hope. What we can rely on is divine presence—in interconnectedness—not intervention. The divine is the power that provides experiences that lead to our evolution, experiences that lead to becoming people of depth, compassion, and wisdom. That happens when we face the givens and say yes to them. The "help of God" does not guarantee safety from the givens but provides support in dealing with them so we can evolve. Our goods may not still be intact, but our goodness is. That is an indicator of grace-full assistance. Divine intervention does not mean that a hand magically changes everything. It means we can still love no matter what happened to us.

A mature prayer is not "Don't let me have to go through this" but "Help me grow through this." Prayer as openness to the graces that come with each given can replace petitions to change or rearrange how the graces should come. Grace is already everywhere doing everything. All we have to do is open to the gift dimension of life. The prayer is yes and thanks. Our attempts to stay in control are denials of grace.

We humans are here on earth as delegates from a higher consciousness, and a simple, thorough yes to reality is how we fulfill our mission. An unswerving loyalty to what is real carries us to the culmination of human consciousness. As Pierre Teilhard de Chardin says: "We tirelessly and ceaselessly search for Something, we know not what, which will appear in the end to those who have penetrated to the very heart of reality." The path to a higher power than ego is saying yes to the predicament we find ourselves in here and now. A religion based on rescuing us from life hobbles and mutes the givens so they cannot impact us fully. Then we lose our best chance at growth.

The givens are *what is*. This has traditionally been called God's will—just the components we need to fulfill the purposes of evolution. "Thy will be done" is the unconditional yes that makes evolution flourish. The ego may find it hard to say, "Not my will but thine be done."

A mature religious consciousness welcomes us to the mysteries in life's uncompromising facts. It is content to let the givens retain an element of mystery rather than explain them away or fend them off. If I ask for an apple, you can show me to the apple tree. If I ask for a shirt, you can get one for me from your dresser. If I ask for your love, where would you go? The most precious realities of human life are beyond our grasp but within the mystery of our hearts. The givens of life are the most long-standing mysteries in human history. Mature religions do not explain them away but honor the mystery by letting it remain somewhat unexplained. *Mystery* comes from a Greek word that also means initiation. A mystery requires not inquiry into solutions but initiation into openings.

Each of the conditions of our existence opens us to features of the world and ourselves that reveal depths that transcend our cognitive powers. The unconditional yes is so much more apt a response than the question why. This is moving from question to choice, from formula to acceptance. Why is for problems that can be solved. Yes is for mysteries in which we become involved. Why makes the givens into problems, and then we look for ways to avoid their full wallop. Yes honors the givens as bedrock reality on which the house of evolution can be built. Both spirituality and religion can help us face our reality and build on it as an adult enterprise.

A religion not geared for adults	*Mature religion or spirituality*
• Insists we follow the voice of authority	• Offers guidance and leaves the decision to us
• Insists on uniformity of beliefs we inherit; we are held to what has already been known	• Respects our unique and new realizations; we enter what we did not know yet
• Proposes clear-cut dogmas and moral codes	• Encourages evolving beliefs that emerge from rather than suppress dialogue

- Becomes fear based: "the loss of heaven and the pains of hell," though it also includes consolations

- Emphasizes compassion and a consoling sense of a loving intent in the universe

- Insists on membership in an institution

- Allows for participatory presence without the need to agree

- Holds the keys to the means of grace and keeps them limited to specific sacraments and rituals

- Offers the power to find, devise, and expand the means of grace without limitation

RELIGION AND REFUGE IN NATURE

On the eighth day of his meditation under the bodhi tree, Siddhartha Gautama suddenly was awakened into the light of consciousness and he exclaimed: "Wonderful world, all things share in enlightened [buddha] nature." Dogen Zenji reports Buddha's words in this thrilling way: "When the morning star appeared, I and the great earth with all its beings, simultaneously became Buddhas."

Siddhartha grasped that the formless light of consciousness is everywhere in every form and given. It is because of our conditioned and obscured ego perception that we fail to notice it. Siddhartha's enlightenment was the recognition that behind the appearances of mortality, both in nature and in ourselves, was something beyond birth and death. Buddha's words echo those of Shakespeare in *The Merchant of Venice:* "Soft stillness and the night become the touches of sweet harmony. . . . Such harmony is in immortal souls, but whilst this muddy vesture of decay [the ego] doth grossly close it in, we cannot hear it."

Buddhism and all religions offer comforting refuges to life's strict directives. These responses are intimately linked to nature. It is significant that Buddha's birth, awakening, and death all happened under trees. Was the bodhi tree merely a backdrop or was it a participant in his awakening? Buddha answers this question clearly when, after being enlightened, he sits for seven days facing the tree to express gratitude to it for its part in his awakening. Nature is a path to the enlightened life.

The central teachings of the Buddha are the universality of suffering, the importance of letting go of attachment, the fact of impermanence, the absence of separateness or of a free-standing self, and the power of the practices of mindfulness and loving-kindness. Nature offers these very same lessons: we and all of nature suffer. Trees let go of their leaves and flowers their petals and we our youth and our very lives. Phases and seasons teach impermanence. Ecology teaches interconnectedness. Opposites combine in twilight and early dawn. Even the practice of loving-kindness is reflected in nature, since nature gives its gifts generously to the wise and the ignorant alike.

The Buddhist teaching that there is no separate self fits Saint Thomas Aquinas's definition of spirituality as "a connectedness with all things." This is an appreciation of nature. The mysticism of Saint Francis also included a realization that natural things are brothers and sisters to us, "brother sun, sister moon." Moreover, in the Christian liturgy, reflecting the Hebrew Bible, are the words: "Heaven *and earth* are full of Thy glory!" (author's emphasis). At the same time, there are elements in traditional religious teaching that disparage nature:

• The natural world is a residence for us humans while we work out our salvation. It is not a means of grace *through* which we are saved or awakened. Nature is only a means to an end.

• Only humans are created in God's image.

• We humans were given dominion over the rest of nature.

• Nature is hierarchically orchestrated in orders and classes of organisms, with man at the top.

• Nature is meant to support us while we use it up, and it is only provisionally valuable, since it will end in fire.

• God created nature and is above it. (When God is male, as in the traditions of Jews, Christians, and Muslims, he creates the world and it is separate from him. When a mythology affirms that a goddess created the world, that world is her own body. For example, Nut is the goddess in Egyptian mythology who swallows the sun at sunset and gives birth to it at dawn, while she herself is the sky.)

John Scotus Erigena, a Catholic theologian of the ninth century, wrote that the "natural world is God as seen by himself." Dogen Zenji, in the thirteenth century, comments on the *Nirvana Sutra:* "All sentient beings have Buddha nature without exception." Thus, for him, natural things possess buddha nature, represent it, and even become epiphanies of it. Dogen appreciated the teaching power of nature: "When you practice correctly, the sounds and forms of the valley streams and the forms and sounds of the mountains all become verses of the sutras. . . . Entreat trees and rocks to preach the Dharma."

In the Islamic tradition, the Koran (45:3–5, 20) says: "Behold in the heavens and on the earth are signs for those who believe. . . . In creation and in all wild creatures, . . . in the alternation of night and day and the sustenance that God sends down from the sky, to revive the earth after its death, and the shifting of the winds are signs for people who understand."

Hindu teacher Sri Aurobindo writes: "Nature's secret process is to reveal essential being through the manifestation of its powers and forms. . . . To become ourselves is the one thing to be done; but the true ourselves is that which is within us, our divine being. . . . It is by growing within . . . that we arrive at the creation of a world which shall be the true environment of divine living. This is the final object that nature has set before us. . . . To be and to be fully is nature's aim in us." Thus nature can be appreciated as a unity of mortality and divinity. We can then enjoy our planet as a most dear and fertile spiritual kingdom. It is a new Jerusalem, the Pure Land of Buddha, the heaven of the saints, a natural nirvana, a sacred refuge.

Evolution moves toward more complexity, that is, more significance, more consciousness. In the course of centuries, that becomes a sense of the personal and then a commitment of personal love, for example, between one person and another. That love then moves outward toward all beings. In this way consciousness is the origin of goodness and evolution is continually moving toward universal love. This happens automatically because we have awakened from the dream of "I am" into the vision of "We are." It is a team approach, and nature is part of our team. Ecology is spirituality is human realization. The "we" is all beings, as was indicated by none other than the strict eighteenth-century New England preacher Jonathan Edwards: "True virtue consists not in love of any particular beings nor in gratitude because they love us, but in a union of our hearts to being in general."

THREE REFUGES

Judaism, Islam, and Christianity refer to God as a refuge. Buddhist teaching offers three refuges when life becomes challenging, three refuges from which we can face the givens of life with courage and wisdom. These are the Buddha, the Dharma, and the Sangha. These are not external forces that somehow protect us from life's pain; rather, they are embodiments of three energies of awakening within us. "Buddha" does not refer to the person who lived in India about twenty-five centuries ago—it is the enlightened mind of any person living now. Buddhism teaches that all of us have buddha nature—that is our essence, whether we're aware of it or not. The Dharma refers to the teachings and practices offered by the Buddha that lead to enlightenment. The Sangha is the community of fellow practitioners on the path to enlightenment.

The three refuges of Buddhism are open to people of any background. Anyone can look to the Buddha as a reminder and an inspiration: Like him, we can awaken to our true nature; we can finally grasp that we have been suffering from an illusion—in reality, we are not separate from one another. The refuge of the Dharma is that of committed spiritual practice, taking up the path of loving-kindness. And in the refuge of Sangha, or community, we share our intention to awaken with others and gain strength in our connectedness with others on the path of wisdom and compassion.

The natural world reflects all three of the refuges. Buddha mind is evident in all that exists in nature. Nature is a vast ecology of interdependencies making it clear to us that nothing stands alone. The

Dharma is the order of reality, and this is visible in nature. And when we spend time in nature, we begin to appreciate that the entire family of living things is our true Sangha.

According to Buddhist tradition, we are all already buddhas, all of us humans and everything in nature. Most of us just do not know who we really are yet. But nature seems to know. In the natural world, reality is continually presented and ruthlessly faced. The Japanese master Dogen Zenji said: "Nature is practicing Buddhism." Nature is always present with what is; nature is always saying yes.

The Buddhist concept of dharma can also be understood as the inner law of things, the laws by which they fulfill themselves and fulfill their role in evolution. The attitude of unconditional yes to the unavoidable challenges of life allows us to fulfill ourselves and grow. In my view, the essence of spiritual practice is cultivating an unconditional yes. The givens of life become gates to enlightenment when we become yes in thought, word, or deed.

The refuge of Sangha, as I've explained, is the group with whom we share a spiritual practice. But sangha can also be our family, a support group, or the people with whom we share important goals or beliefs. We feel a camaraderie with them as we pursue our path together. We trust their support and give them ours. *Can we learn to lean?* We are committed to sharing our life experiences with our fellow sangha members, and in doing this, we announce that we are not discrete beings but interconnected and interactive beings.

The three refuges we find in Buddhism are three sparks that fire us up, three encouraging graces that make us bearers of light, three pushes to help us leap. This is why they are referred to as three jewels, that is, three valuable treasures on the spiritual path. A poetic aspiration (with some humor):

May the pterodactyl of insuperable dharma
Pounce upon my slippery ego
And pick it clean
In the aerie of inescapable enlightenment.

DISTRACTION OR RESOURCE?

Some refuges are helpful; some can hurt us. Some are not appropriate; some are "weekend appropriate." Occasional shopping sprees, occasional drinking, does not mean perdition. Only when they become addictive are they dangerous. I am convinced that a spiritual practice is important in the process of recovery from addiction. However, the skillful means toward recovery are manifold, not single. Beings as complex as we require all the help we can get. I have found that twelve-step programs offer a reliable path to recovery, especially when they are supported by therapy and spiritual practices.

Some refuges are distractions and some are resources. Part of adult spirituality is having the wisdom to know the difference. Drugs distract; a hike in nature grants a resource. Positive resourceful refuges are relationships, friendships, art, nature, music, creativity, career, entertainment, meditation, and the variety of nonhurtful ways we have of fulfilling our own deepest needs and wishes.

For so many of us, the serene resourceful refuges of Buddhism—Buddha, Dharma, and Sangha—do not stand a chance against the refuges that offer adrenaline-rich excitement or a visit to the shores of Lethe, the mythic river of forgetful distraction. Indeed, a person may sometimes go so far as to say: "Well, I can always commit suicide to solve my problems. I give myself that out." As long as we have that option, we need never be motivated to use all our creative ingenuity to face life's sometimes depressing dilemmas. A relationship to Buddha or Christ or to nature itself helps us give up that sheltering but destructive option. Shakespeare states such a healthy surrender in *King Lear:*

> You ever-gentle gods, take my breath
>   from me;
> Let not my worser spirit tempt me again
> To die before you please.

It is no coincidence that the twenty-third Psalm is recited at fu-nerals rather than at weddings. Perhaps someone noticed that "green pastures" and "still waters" were not so appealing to the living. To choose the refuges offered on the spiritual path means giving up al-tered states and escapist diversions in favor of life as it is. Resting in that reality endows us with a composure that many of us would find extremely boring. "I doubt sometimes whether a quiet and unagi-tated life would have suited me—yet I sometimes long for it," Lord Byron wrote. I believe that most of us act in accord with that state-ment, though we say we definitely want serenity.

Sabbath rest can happen in any moment in which we are not driven or stopped by fear or desire. We often prefer the drama, the storms of fear and desire, the uncertainty and confusion that come with complicated relationships and choices. This inclination is not al-together negative. Stress and uproar, in small doses, can be creative and can even catapult us into new possibilities. They can stir our imagination and incite us to move enthusiastically toward new hori-zons. We are summoned to spend some time at the fair and some time in the pastures. It may also be true that when we go headlong into what we repressed before, we are yearning to integrate it. We go mad to become sane sometimes.

MAGICAL THINKING

In the face of life's givens, we might take refuge in superstitious thoughts or magical rituals of safety we devise to protect ourselves from what we fearfully believe is a scary, unpredictable, and punitive world. This is magical thinking, using our wishes or fears to explain what is happening or can happen. It hearkens from our collective primitive sense of danger and its consequent illusions. We mistake a feared or desired connection for a real one. Here are some examples of magical thinking:

• Reality will become or remain the same as my mental picture of it.

- Dangerous forces will erupt if I do not adhere to very precise rules or rituals.
- Something has always been wrong with me and I cannot know or fix it—though everyone else is aware of it.
- I have been guilty from early life and still have not been fully punished.
- We get what we deserve.
- I am eternally indebted. I always owe something to God or have to keep paying for something I have done that remains unfixably wrong.
- If it had not been for this one thing happening or if one special thing would happen, everything would be perfect now.
- Need fulfillment is scarce, so I must work hard and consider myself lucky to find some satisfaction.
- I have to grasp this opportunity right now or lose it. There is no time for a mindful pause.
- If people knew me as I really am, they would not love me or want me.
- "What goes around, comes around." This is a wish of the frustrated retaliatory ego, not a karmic certainty.
- If I do not remain in control, everything will fall apart.
- The spiritual realm does not exist since it cannot be confirmed by scientific methods, i.e., it cannot be controlled. (Disbelief is often a control issue.)
- If I bring an issue out into the open, it will become even more serious and dangerous. If I never mention it, it will go away.
- Happiness will not last if I enjoy it too much. Full-on exuberance is dangerous.
- Prosperity will be followed by catastrophe: "A bull market has a bear behind it" and vice versa.
- There is a by-and-by to come in history in which there will be no violence or evil and the human shadow will disappear.

Allied to magical thinking is wishful thinking. For example, I expect everything to be better in the future, though I am doing nothing to make that happen. I believe the economy will improve very soon.

Such self-deceptions are wishful-thinking based, not reality based. Once we are adults, nothing satisfies but the truth of what is real, however lackluster or unappealing. A yes to the facts of life means an attitude of "give it to me straight."

BACKSTREET REFUGES

When we are afraid of the givens of our existence, we take refuge in our most childish hideouts. It can be the absolute certainties of religion or the escape hatch of addiction. It can be anything that grants distraction and consolation. In the fear-based arena, we lose track of our authentic needs and wishes. *Authentic* is from a Greek word meaning "self-doer," and thus like the Latin word *author*, so to be authentic is to be the author of our needs and wishes. They do not mimic those of others, nor are they forced on us by others. We speak as authorities.

For many of us, no matter what our stated beliefs, our real refuges are not God or nature or the Buddha, the Dharma, and the Sangha. Our refuges in the face of stress, conflict, or inner turmoil might be alcohol, food, sex, drugs, gambling, shopping, and so forth. Or we might take refuge in our intellect. We may do this in two ways. We deny what happened, or the impact of what happened, or we make excuses for what happened so that we do not have to feel anything in response. This is a denial of the unconditional yes to whatever painful facts of life have arisen. Second, we may put our energy into thinking things through with the use of our analytical powers. This too can be based on a fear of the full impact of our feelings. Perhaps we still do not trust the experience of mindfulness, with its careful and sane attention to reality, without the distractions and consolations the intellect contrives.

People become more contactful toward us when we show our vulnerabilities. This may be why we hide our feelings. In my own life, I can see that I often hide the feelings that would make me more appealing. I avoid letting others see how bereft, scared, or needy I really feel sometimes. I am hiding the fact that one of the givens—suffering is part of life—applies to a "big shot" like me. This is the opposite of going to a spiritual practice, to the members of a sangha or religious or social community, to a therapist or friend, to show my feelings and find help to work things out or at least someone to witness my pain. To take refuge in the pretensions constructed by my ego mind is the opposite of going to my own inner strength or to my enlightened mind, higher Self, or Buddha or Christ within, which would enjoin mindfulness, direct attention to reality, without indulging in the intellectual machinations that are tailored to avoid it.

I can also see that I will go to food when I am facing a painful reality. I will overeat or snack or seek comfort foods. I console myself with eating rather than opening myself to the refuges that spiritual practice serves up. Or when something is depressing me, I will stop eating or eat very little. My appetite is trained after all these years to reflect my moods. It is not trained to go directly to the three jewels of Buddhism or to the values offered in religion. In my childhood, eating was a refuge and ritual. Food was not fuel; it was an answer. If I told Grandma I felt glum, she would say, "Have some eggplant parmigiana and you'll feel better." I do not blame my past or my relatives, only notice how my origins oriented me toward the refuges I still, mistakenly, believe are reliable.

In childhood, religion was definitely a refuge too. The beauty of Catholic rituals, with all their sensual delights, was enormously seductive. The smell of beeswax and incense, the colors of the vestments and images, the sounds of the chants and hymns, the taste and touch of the sacraments, provided tangible evidence that the church offered a sanctuary from the world as given. I could go there whenever I felt needy or sad or scared. Indeed, a title of the Virgin Mary is Refuge of Sinners. I appreciate the riches of my religious past and hope to develop my religious consciousness further. Our work is not to toss it all out but to find what is good and expand on it.

SAFETY IN NO REFUGE

*Only when all the crutches and props are broken . . . and
there is no hope for security, does it become possible to experience . . . the archetype of meaning.*

—C. G. JUNG

The five givens are scary to most of us. We are threatened by the
thought that what we cherish will be lost. We are afraid that our plans
will fall through. We are threatened by unfairness and the suffering
that happens in life. We are afraid of how people may hurt us.

We hope for a refuge or guarantee of safety in the face of the conditions of existence. Refuges can be yes oriented or no oriented. They are
negative when they provide escape and positive when they open us to
and equip us for reality as it is. The three refuges in Buddhism are resources that recommend full presence in reality, neither adorned nor
armored with our mental elaborations. The shelter that mindfulness
offers is that of safety in no escape. No escape for the ego means victory
for our buddha nature, our true identity.

In the last months of his life, the Buddha said to his disciples:
"Take refuge in yourselves and not in anything else. In you are the
Buddha, the Dharma, and the Sangha. Do not look for things far be-
yond you. Everything is in your own heart."

The central purpose of taking refuge in any adult spiritual practice
is to go into our experience, in whatever shape it has taken. We let
ourselves feel it all, be in it as it is, and we do not try to change or fix
or end it. We let it take its own time to play itself out. We let it take
us down or up. This is precisely what is recommended in state-of-the-
art psychology today: to find resolution through full entry into our experience no matter how painful. To go into fear and to come out the
other end is a path that many conscious people are finally beginning
to walk.

We cannot take refuge in feeling good, because that cannot be sustained. What is sustained and sustaining is a yes to what is, "taking
the good with the bad." This can only happen when we have no

attachment to how things should be. No notions have weight except those that accurately mirror reality. Perhaps this is what Tibetan meditation master Chögyam Trungpa means when he says: "Good, bad, happy, sad, vanish like the imprint of a bird in the sky."

Finally, this is not a one-way street. Buddha and Christ also take refuge in us, since they need us in order to become alive in our world. The light of wisdom and compassion happens only when individuals act with compassion and wisdom. It is the mystery of the Incarnation: timeless spiritual powers activate in the world of time through individuals. Being reaches us in beings—and we are those beings. Refuge is thus directly related to the highest of human possibilities: to have the same heart in us that is in Jesus or Buddha, to become in our lifetime what they were in theirs. As Dogen says: "This birth and death [the cycle of samsara] is quite a suitable path to the Buddha mind." I am God's and Buddha's personal disclosure.

I notice that I still visit my old favorite refuges. But my new practice is to pause, even for a moment, and look in a mindful way at what I am doing. I am then more and more apt to put aside my habitual refuges and ask for new refuges, the ones that offer more reliability. We may not always be able honestly to declare a commitment to the three refuges of Buddhism or to the refuges in our religious tradition, but we can always aspire to them.

WISDOM WITHIN US

C. G. Jung proposed a concept of a treasury of the collective psyche into which individuals throughout the ages deposit their individuated experiences and their personal wisdom. Every wise realization of any human creates an ever-richer collective granary from which all can draw, an example of interconnectedness. This same concept of a treasury of merits or graces is found in Catholic theology and relates to the doctrine of the communion of saints, the interconnectedness of all beings, living and dead. In this universal consciousness there is no dualism of past and present, since all the riches of wisdom are available at every moment. Every grace that comes to us as individuals is from a collective heritage. This is the positive dimension of karma. We all help one another work through our karma. We are refuges to one another.

The source and the harvest of religious wisdom are stored in the silo of our own souls. When sages and saints share their insights with us, they are expressing a universal wisdom that is always and already in us. When we are stirred by scriptures or sutras, we are hearing the rumbling of our own immemorial intelligence. The stirring is from within. As Jung says: "Statements made in the Holy Scriptures are also utterances of the soul."

We are a mystical body of humanity. Each new or found revelation and intuition triggers hitherto untapped coding in all of us. When enough of us come to the font of wisdom with an unconditional yes, a vast perspective opens for the collective. This interdependent transformation happens in a much more expansive way than can come from personal meditation or personal affirmations. The more people enter spiritual consciousness, the sooner the rest of the world follows suit. The more widespread the unconditional yes, the more the evolutionary advance. In that sense, we are each individual mediators of grace to the world, and so much depends on our yes.

Our life then is a gift, a grace we received from ancestral others, like our own bodies. Our natural response to what is given is pure gratitude. This thankfulness is a yes to our connectedness. It is also the pathway to offering all that we do for the benefit of our fellow humans. Indeed, gratitude is the bridge between the practice of loving-kindness and taking up the saints' and bodhisattvas' unconditionally loving way of life.

I take refuge in unconditional love, eternal wisdom, and healing power here in my heart and in others' hearts, all one heart of the universe.

PART TWO

AN UNCONDITIONAL YES TO OUR CONDITIONED EXISTENCE

I found in the writings of those great medieval mystics, for whom self-surrender had been the way to self-realization . . . that they had found the strength to say Yes to every demand which the needs of their neighbors had made them face, and to say Yes also to every fate life had in store for them. . . . They found an unreserved acceptance of life, whatever it brought them personally of toil, suffering, or happiness.

—Dag Hammarskjöld, *Markings*

SEVEN

HOW TO BECOME YES

THE WORD *yes* sums up spirituality and sanity. An unconditional yes to what is frees us from the self-imposed suffering that results when we fear facing the givens of life. Yes is born of trust and heals fear. This is because we are acknowledging that whatever happens to us is part of our story and useful on our path. Our yes to the conditions of existence means getting on with life rather than being caught up in dispute and in attempts to gain control of how things play out.

When things change and end, we become trusting of the cycles of life as steps to evolutionary growth. Yes alleviates our suffering by freeing us from clinging to anything at all. When things do not go according to our plans, we stretch our potential for trusting a power beyond our ego. Our ego's futile and ferocious attempts to make everything come out its own way give way to letting the chips fall where they may. Yes frees us from the suffering caused by the compulsion to be in charge.

When things are not fair, we evoke our potential to act fairly no matter what. This means trusting a power beyond our ego, with all its insistence on retaliation and its petulant demands for equity. A yes to this third given frees us from the suffering that happens when we are caught up in getting back at people and when we hold grudges. When pain enters our life, we activate our potential for facing it without complaint, and we gain compassion for others who also suffer. A yes to this fourth given frees us from the suffering that comes from useless protest. When people are not loyal or loving toward us, we enliven our potential for unconditional love. A yes frees us from the suffering caused by our need to hurt or reject those who have disappointed us.

Fear is a no to what is. To fear the givens is to be afraid of life, since they are its components. Fear prevents us from experiencing life fully and living in the moment by creating avoidance and attraction. We avoid what is unpleasant and we grasp at whatever makes us feel good. The Buddhist tradition encourages us to take a middle path. The chart on page 103 shows the work that installs us in this "golden mean," as the ancient Romans called it.

Each condition of existence thus equips us with a handy skill. Since it is a given that people leave us, it becomes a given that we will be alone, so it is wise to plan for that by becoming comfortable being by ourselves right now. Since it is a given that things do not always go according to plan, it is a given that we will be disappointed, so it is wise to become comfortable with fewer expectations. Since it is a given that things are not always fair, it is a given that we will occasionally feel cheated, so it is wise to become comfortable with grieving losses, with working for justice, and with letting go of the urge to retaliate. Since it is a given that pain is part of life, it is a given that we will do best to become comfortable with bearing it and growing because of it. Since it is a given that people are not always loyal and loving, it is wise to let go of censure and become committed to loving-kindness no matter how others may treat us.

Yes to life's givens thus combines defenselessness with resourcefulness. Yes means we are open to the events that befall us, defenseless in the face of them. At the same time, we are not bowled over by what happens to us. We are resourceful in dealing with them; we do all we can to handle the givens we face. Then we let the chips fall where they may. Soon we pick them up one by one and place our bets again.

There is a vitality in us, a sparkle—a bonfire, actually—that cannot be extinguished by any tragedy. Something in us, an urge toward wholeness, a passion for evolving, makes us go on, start over, not give up, not give in. To accept the things we cannot change does not mean

The Given	Our Fear in the Face of It	How We Mask Our Fear	The Yes That Fits Best
Things change and end.	We may lose what we have.	Being less committed or becoming stoical.	Grieve and let go.
Things don't always go according to plan.	Our expectations will not be met.	Plan every detail and try to stay in control.	Accept what happens and learn from it.
Things are not always fair.	We might not get our fair share.	Insist on keeping everything even and blame those who are unfair.	Have an attitude of "You win some; you lose some" while working for justice.
Pain is part of life.	We will not be able to handle it.	Try to be on guard to avoid pain.	Allow pain that is natural and do not add to pain by attempting to control it.
People are not loving and loyal all the time.	We will feel hurt and have to grieve.	Stay away from closeness in the future.	Speak up and say "Ouch!" while not retaliating.

that we roll over but that we roll on. Openness and creative resource-fulness happen synchronously each time we are confronted with one of the givens. Some people write their best poems when they suffer.

The practice of an unconditional yes is the heart of the ancient spiritual tradition of Taoism. *Wu wei* is a Taoist term meaning to go with the flow of things as they are. This reduces the friction and stress that arise when we resist reality as it wants to happen. In my view, the ancient spiritual teachings and practices of Taoism form a technology of cultivating an unconditional yes to life's givens.

The Taoist teacher Han Hung wrote, "The biggest risk is to trust that these conditions are all that we need to be ourselves." This is a profound realization of the connection between our unconditional yes and our trust that the conditions of existence are precisely what we need for personal growth and fulfillment. The givens of life show us who we really are and help us be the best we can be:

- Only in changes and endings do we find out how we hold on or let go.
- Only in failed plans do we find out about a larger plan afoot that has our best interests at heart, trusting the heartfulness of the universe and discovering our spiritual potential.
- Only when things are not fair do we find our dark side, which seeks retaliation, or our kindly side, which looks for restoration and lets go if it cannot happen.
- Only when we suffer do we find our courage and our depth and learn compassion for others' suffering.
- Only when others are disloyal and unloving do we find out if we can really love unconditionally.

LOVING-KINDNESS

An unconditional yes is a spiritual victory. There are spiritual prac-tices that help us reach it. These practices make it easier to live with our givens instead of against them.

A useful practice is to see all the events of our lives and all the conditions we meet up with as dharmas, doors into enlightenment, lessons in humanity, paths to virtue. Each of the givens offers a spiritual challenge. When things change or end, we can grieve and let go rather than shake our fist at heaven. When things do not go according to plan, we can open to new possibilities, some from destiny, some from karma. When things prove unfair, we can work for justice and not retaliate against others but focus on their transformation. When suffering comes our way, we can experience it without protest or blame or the demand that we be exempted. When others are not loving or loyal, we can practice loving-kindness. In the face of any given we say yes mindfully, that is, without the mind-sets of ego.

Our mindfulness practice culminates in loving-kindness. In this book I mention loving-kindness many times. It is a virtue we love to give and receive. Now we can look at loving-kindness as a specific Buddhist practice by which we show our hospitality to humanity. This practice is based on a Buddhist text called the *Metta Sutta*. *Metta* is a Pali term used in Theravadin Buddhism meaning love, the energy that resides in and activates the universe, all-inclusive and unconditional. Loving-kindness is the widest unconditional yes because it is a love that includes the whole universe.

The teaching of metta implies unconditional love as a remedy for fear of others and as an honoring of the way they differ from us. Metta is an unconditional friendliness toward ourselves and others, with a willingness to allow the expression of any of our own or others' feelings and experiences without interpretation, blame, or censorship. The practice of loving-kindness presupposes that we are all interconnected and helps make that fact conscious and real in the moment.

In the Buddhist view, four boundless realms of consciousness drive our spiritual lives. These four spiritual potentials in us—givens of our nature—are love, compassion, sympathetic joy, and equanimity. Since they exist within us no matter what our circumstances, that is, unconditionally, they are referred to as the "four immeasurables" or "divine abidings."

Love involves an unconditional intention and will that all beings be well and happy. Compassion means being touched by the pain others feel and wanting them to be free of suffering. Sympathetic joy wishes that all have good fortune and rejoices when others are successful. Equanimity is serenity and groundedness in all circumstances, no longer being halted or compelled by fear or desire, memory or anticipation. Equanimity does not mean that there will be no upheavals in life but that we develop our ability to go through difficulties without being devastated or becoming embittered. In other words, we can relate to them rather than be possessed by them. We still feel the impact of upheavals, but we always come back to center and ground. As T. S. Eliot says in his poem "Ash Wednesday":

> Teach us to care and not to care
> Teach us to sit still
> Even among these rocks.

The practice of loving-kindness activates and cultivates these four immeasurable virtues in our lives. It awakens our full potential of human goodness because it helps us love more, our crowning virtue. *Immeasurable* does not mean large but impartial, not limited to one target. It is felt in equal depth for all beings, liked and unliked, known and unknown, near and far. Loving-kindness is our way of responding with a yes to the givens of life as others suffer them. It is thus also a way of loving ourselves, since we become more lovable as we love others.

The practice of loving-kindness means expanding our spiritual purpose consciously so that our heart includes with equal force those we love, those to whom we are indifferent, those with whom we have difficulties, and all beings everywhere. Thus the affirmation "I listen to nature and am open to its healing power in my life" is only the first level of a spiritually mature practice. We enrich our practice of loving others when a personal affirmation is followed by aspirations that it apply to all beings: "May those I love listen to nature and be open to its healing power in their lives. . . . May those with whom I have difficulty listen to nature and be open to its healing power in their lives. . . . May all humans listen to nature and be open to its healing power in their lives." Indeed, with this as a model, we can choose no longer to have purely personal spiritual practices; they can all be tailored to include everyone. As we arise from the meditation pillow, we might say: "By the power of this and all my practices may all beings find the path of compassion and wisdom."

Here are some instructions based on the Buddhist practice of loving-kindness:

Breathe normally, focusing attention on each breath. Let go of thoughts and make room for the powers ready to come through you. Picture yourself as a person of compassion, then of love, then of joy, then of equanimity. These qualities are called the "four immeasurables" because they are the abundant driving forces of your buddha nature.

Say aloud or internally your aspiration that people give and receive these four gifts. In this way you beam the gifts, which come not from you but through you from the heart of Buddha, Christ, the universe. Ask for the gift of compassion for those who love you, for those whom you love, for your benefactors, for friends, and for acquaintances. Next, include people you don't know well but meet in daily life, such as merchants and service people. Next, beam compassion to people who do not like you, to those whom you dislike, to difficult people, to hostile people, and to enemies (both personal and political). Finally, beam compassion to the whole world—north, south, east, and west. Now repeat your imaging of the same ever-widening circle as you beam love, joy, and then equanimity.

Here is an example of how it sounds: "May those I love give and receive compassion today," "May those with whom I have difficulty give and receive joy today." Here is an alternative style: "May all my enemies have joy here and now. . . . May all my acquaintances have equanimity. . . . May they be free from suffering and the causes of suffering."

Pay attention to any resistance you feel. Do not try to eliminate the resistance. Simply work on building a stronger intention to love, and the resistance will lighten. You are expressing your true nature, and this may threaten your ego with its highly limited preferences and exclusions. This practice is a yes to the immeasurably inclusive compassion, love, joy, and equanimity that your healthy ego longs to feel.

The practice of loving-kindness can be applied to people who have hurt or criticized us in the past and whose voices still impact our self-confidence in negative ways. "May he become enlightened so that he can help others instead of hurting them." This makes a hurtful person milder in our minds. When we instead say: "May he be hurt as he hurt me," we make the person into a jailer who goes on detaining us.

Loving-kindness can apply to our mind's activities too. For instance, memories that suddenly arise in us can be felt as flowers or arrows. Some are happy, some painful or even regretful. Whenever a memory arises, we can attach a loving-kindness practice to it. For instance, you suddenly recall a time when your mother did not stand up for you. Add a loving-kindness practice by saying, "May my mother and all mothers learn to stand up for their children." You recall how your mother comforted you when you were sad. "May I comfort my mother when she needs it. May all sons comfort their mothers. May all of us find comfort in mother nature."

TONGLEN PRACTICE

A related Buddhist meditation practice is tonglen. *Tong* means sending out, and *len* means bringing in. We can also think of this meditation practice as letting go and letting in. Tonglen is rooted in mindfulness and loving-kindness and is meant to free us from self-centeredness.

The practice has three phases. First is a mindful quietude: For a few moments, sit quietly and tune in to your innate serenity. The second phase of tonglen is practicing taking in and sending out. With each in-breath we imagine ourselves breathing in dark qualities such as pain, constriction, and heat. Then with the out-breath we send out light, openness, coolness. We consciously feel these qualities moving in and out of our entire bodies. Do this for several minutes.

The third phase is to continue taking in and sending out, moving your attention to any emotional pain you may be feeling in the moment. Breathe in the qualities of that pain, and breathe out peace, openness, coolness, and the like. After doing this for some time, you can then follow the same arc as in the loving-kindness practice. Begin with yourself and then expand your practice to a friend or loved one. Think of a friend who is suffering, breathe in that suffering, and breathe out peace. As you breathe in and out in this way, you are acting like a filter, taking in what is painful, transforming it within yourself, and sending out openness and light.*

This is a challenging meditation practice. After you have practiced it for some time, you can expand your practice past yourself and your loved ones to your acquaintances, your enemies, and finally the whole world. For instance, if we start our practice from a place of feeling desperate and afraid, we can ultimately breathe in the desperation and fears of all and breathe out love and courage. This is how we can begin to feel interconnectedly.

This entire practice is a paradox because it seems to be dangerous to let in what is so undesirable. But acting as bodhisattvas and saints now, we trust that we have access to the abundant stores of light and healing in our buddha nature. We trust that we can let in the pain and not be hurt by it and that we can exude goodness and heal by it.

This is a daring practice and one that connects us to others in abiding ways. It is a form of heartful compassion. Tonglen practice is related directly to the givens of life:

• We breathe in the experience of grief and loss that come with change and endings others are feeling, and we breathe out release from and resolution of them.
• We breathe in others' disappointment because of failed plans and breathe out trust that things will work out for spiritual progress.

---

*For more instruction on tonglen meditation practice, see Pema Chödrön's book *Start Where You Are* or *The Compassion Box* (the audio program in this box features further instruction and a guided tonglen meditation).

- We breathe in the unfairness and injustice others are facing, and we breathe out courage to stand up to injustice and to act justly toward others while remaining nonretaliatory.
- We breathe in physical and psychological suffering and breathe out healing and serenity.
- We breathe in the hurt all humans feel when others are disloyal or unloving, and we breathe out love and loyalty.

An example of combining our practice of loving-kindness and tonglen is to become aware of a sense of community with others—"communion of saints"—in the world who feel or have felt as we do. Whatever pain or stress we face, others have faced it too. It may help to add this to all our personal work on ourselves: "As I feel this, I now join with all those who are facing this same pain or conflict. I ask their help and I share my graces with them." "I join with other depressed people everywhere in this moment. I ask that we release one another from unhappiness." In this way we can make both a deposit and a withdrawal from the repository of graces in which we all share.

These practices can free us from self-centeredness and open us to grace. We are not *achieving* anything. We are *opening* ourselves and becoming windows that let the light of enlightened consciousness through. It flows through us when we breathe in the sufferings of the world and breathe out a healing response. We are not the healers, only the mediators of healing. Grace means access to a power beyond ego. Grace works best when we do our practices, yet it is not caused by them, only coaxed by them.

Loving-kindness and tonglen practice confuse and shock the ego, with its penchant toward retaliation as a tried and true answer to the blows others inflict on us. When we choose to practice loving-kindness and tonglen, we shake the foundations of ego and cause cracks in its hard shell. Through these fissures dawns the light of wisdom and compassion. This warms and brightens the ego's path, and the ego becomes more tender. It loves finding such a wonderful alternative to its favorite sports of fear, attachment, control, and entitlement. The practices of loving-kindness and tonglen help us find the grace not only to transcend ego but to grant it peace.

NO OUTSIDE

Often in this book I've taken the position of "both . . . and" rather than "either . . . or." This is a way of referring to a marvelous possibility: the combination of apparent opposites. Our ego loves to divide and conquer, but our spiritual consciousness thrives on cutting through dualism. "Both . . . and" is paradox, the mind's way of expressing the nondual nature of reality. Metaphors can serve the same purpose.

In dualistic religious perspectives, we pray to a God who is in a heaven above us. In mature religious consciousness, we realize there is no duality, no difference between outside and inside. This has been made especially clear in the mystical elements of all the world's religions. Mystics experience spiritual wisdom rather than receive it from mediators. Mystics cut through literalisms to metaphorical appreciations of reality. An example of nonduality, in Christian theology, is the doctrine of the communion of saints. This refers to the continuing bond between the saints who have finished their earthly journey and those of us still here in the midst of it. God and the saints are here in us and we invoke them for help. Thus interconnectedness is a happening "on earth as it is in heaven." Even after our last breath, we go on showing compassion and sharing wisdom. Thus there is no division between life and death. The communion of saints shows that our evolutionary destiny does not end with death. This is another way of saying that death is not the end of the cycle of life but part of it.

One of the key "saints" of the Buddhist tradition is Avalokiteshvara, the bodhisattva of compassion. Like all gods and saints, Avalokiteshvara is not actually a supreme being above or beyond us but is rather a quality *inside* us. When we act with compassion, or show love, we are acting in accord with our own inborn potential for awakening in any moment. Wisdom and engaged compassion are both practices and fruits of practice.

A bodhisattva is an enlightened being who has vowed to bring all beings with her or him into enlightenment. The practice of lovingkindness is a way of living out the commitment of a bodhisattva. We may not be able to heal people completely by this practice, but we can generate a kind of spiritual alert in the universe of the bodhisattvas who work for the ultimate benefit of all of us. In the Buddhist conception, there are many bodhisattvas at work in and for our world—like the Christian, Jewish, and Muslim saints. In a sense, through spiritual practices such as loving-kindness and tonglen, we join with the bodhisattvas who work with and for all beings. When we think of our spiritual practice in this way, we dislodge our sense of limitation and our impatience with our inadequacy in helping others. Indeed, as we arise from the meditation pillow we might say: "I am thankful to all the buddhas and bodhisattvas that have joined me in this meditation."

NATURE PRACTICES YES

Yes is openness. Nature opens itself to everyone without discrimination. This universal generosity happens to us when we awaken to loving-kindness. Likewise, nature does not retaliate. The man who litters the beach may nonetheless catch a fish the same day.

The origin of the practice of loving-kindness in Buddhist tradition directly relates to nature. It is said that Buddha sent some young monks into the forest to set up a practice center. They soon came running back because they were afraid of the forest spirits who frightened and opposed them. Buddha told them to go back and sit in the midst of the dark spirits and show loving-kindness to them. He taught the monks the metta practice, that is, to show love for those we hate or fear by aspiring that they find the four immeasurables—love, compassion, sympathetic joy, and equanimity. The monks did this, and the spirits were so touched by the loving-kindness practice that they became allies and guides. The practice of loving-kindness is precisely how fear is transformed into love. When we fear anyone, we surround the person with love and our fear becomes love. As Saint John of the Cross says: "Where there is no love put love and you will find love."

Nature is such a great resource in living yes: the model of yes and the gift of yes. Looking at a flower and honoring it as a guide, not just as something beautiful, helps us relate to nature in a creative way. This kind of upgrade in consciousness is how the subtle guidance from nature unfolds. A flower becomes a symbol of the tender life in us that can only grow by firm anchoring to the earth, by welcoming the seasons, and by passing without complaint through its phases. Then a rose is not just a rose but an escort to rebirth.

Japanese Zen poet Ryokan writes: "If your heart is pure, then all things in the world are pure. . . . And the moon and flowers will guide you on your path." In this metaphor nature is compared to a guide. This implies that we are not alone in attempting to be the best humans we can be. Nature can appear as a guiding energy that is continually supporting us in that purpose. Then we can be glad to become a refugee from ego's barren land.

Egolessness thus means bringing the spaciousness of the earth and sky into our sense of what we are. We feel a sense of conjunction to the universe rather than maintaining a limited view of ourselves as separate. Egolessness means having a beginner's mind. The inference is that we can rely on nature as an ever-copious source of graces the more we let go of ego. These graces are in the wonders we see: flowers, mountains, the moon, other humans. They are the equivalent of guardian angels, or bodhisattvas, beings of light who guide us in finding the light in ourselves and in the universe.

Ryokan's lines offer an additional metaphor—and promise—of becoming a guide to others when we are pure intentioned, that is, wanting what is best for others. We are always out for higher stakes in spiritual consciousness. Metaphors can be more than personal. They are also collective. We, and all the things in nature, carry a personal history and the history of the world in ourselves. A metaphor about being a guide to individuals, therefore, can also tell us of our evolutionary purpose of providing guidance for planetary unfolding. We do not have to be world leaders to pull this off. All it takes is yes to the what is of our life today.

Scientist Ilya Prigogine says: "Today the world we see outside and the world we see within are converging." To look within is not meant to oppose our being out in nature. It is now clear that an *engaged* spirituality requires work in the world in a politically active role and simultaneously some distance from the workaday world in a contemplative mode. This contemplation can happen in nature. We can go to the water or the woods for a time out and find spiritual refreshment as depicted in the twenty-third Psalm: "Green pastures . . . still waters . . . restore my soul." As Dogen Zenji says: "Delusion happens when we see all that is from the viewpoint of the self. Enlightenment happens when we see ourselves from the viewpoint of the things in nature."

Here are some specific ways to ally ourselves with nature in an unconditional yes:

• Make it a point from time to time to watch the sun rise and set, as well as the moon rising and setting. Do not simply look at the moon but have a favorite viewing place for each phase. Look at the night sky and become sensitive to the subtle movements there. In ancient times it was believed that the heavenly bodies made music as they moved. This was called the music of the spheres. Attend to that music and hum with it.

• Dreams give answers to questions we have not yet learned to ask. Go camping more often and sleep outdoors so that the stars above can radiate their light into your dreams.

• You may dream about an animal. It is useful, upon awakening, to follow that animal in your imagination. Animals often appear in dreams to show us a path beyond ego. We see this in Alice following the white rabbit or in Dorothy following her dog Toto. A new world opened to them when they let animals take the lead.

• Poems often flow from life's mysterious givens. Feed your soul by reading and writing poetry, listening to music, looking at art, drawing or sculpting, and engaging in any other soul-nurturing arts that are available to you. Do all this outdoors whenever possible. Basho, the Japanese haiku poet, wrote: "No matter what we may be doing at a given moment, it has a bearing on our everlasting self which is poetry."

• Open yourself to the realization that nature is always communicating with you. Look at natural things and hearken to messages that are addressing your immediate condition or the issues facing you.

When a creature or flower appears suddenly or surprisingly or in a place that is unusual, such a visit may have a message for you and may be addressing your immediate life condition. Some Native Americans use the phrase "animal [or flower] medicine" when this happens.

> We consider bibles and religions divine . . .
> . . . they have all grown out of you, and may
>   grow out of you still.
> It is not they who give the life, it is you who
>   give the life,
> Leaves are not more shed from the trees, or
>   trees from
> The earth, than they are shed out of you.
> —WALT WHITMAN,
> "SONG FOR OCCUPATIONS,"
> FROM *Leaves of Grass*

May I practice loving-kindness in all my dealings, and may those who act with hate become so free of fear that love becomes all they know or show.

EIGHT

YES TO FEELINGS

Speak what we feel, not what we ought to say.
—WILLIAM SHAKESPEARE, *King Lear*

THE WORD *feeling* comes from an Indo-European root meaning "touch." There is a term in science, *perturbation,* which refers to the ability of natural things to experience change and movement. This is what makes for evolution and the flow of life. To feel is to activate our capacity to be touched, moved, and changed by events, nature, and people—by the givens of our existence.

We can be pushed and crushed by life's pressures or we can become fair and alert witnesses of them and then choose the next best thing to do. Witnessing our feelings about and our reactions to circumstances means not being caught up in them, not taking them too personally or too seriously, not being possessed by them, not being devastated by them, not being stopped or driven by them. Our spiritual purpose is not to repress or indulge our emotions but to allow them so fully that they move through us and go to ground, that is, are resolved—or even go back to earth, as we will.

When we live life with an unconditional yes, we develop equanimity. But equanimity is not to be construed as imperturbability. Equanimity is the virtue of returning to baseline, restabilizing, after we feel the perturbation aroused by our feelings. People who are healthy both psychologically and spiritually are touched by what happens to them and to others. They are impacted by events. They feel deeply and they show it. They are not immovable or stoical about what others do or about what happens. They are penetrable. Otherwise, how could the light come through them?

Character, depth, and compassion bloom in us *because* we can be impacted by what happens to us. But events do not have to impinge upon our lives in dangerous ways:

When events impact, a person	*When events impinge, a person*
• Feels feelings safely, remaining grounded and centered	• Is overwhelmed by feelings, becoming destabilized and devastated
• Goes through the experience consciously and seeks healthy support at the same time	• Uses drugs or some addiction to escape or avoid reality
• Notices that sleep and appetite are affected moderately	• Notices that sleep and appetite are affected seriously
• Addresses, processes, and resolves the issue	• Gets stuck in obsessive dead-end thoughts and continues to feel the pummel of events
• Feels down, but at a level appropriate to the situation	• Is depressed or in despair*
• Maintains physical health	• Damages physical health

---

*Despair is a given, but not necessarily a nemesis, of every human life. It is a giving up on ourselves, on others, and on grace: We believe, correctly or incorrectly, that we have no holding environment of support, visible or invisible. We sense an irreparable disconnect. We notice that our reaching out or our getting angry has no effect on events or on others. We feel a pervasive powerlessness, a lack of a sense of agency and efficacy. We give up on ourselves because what we have tried has not worked. Perhaps our obsession with being in control is our touching and so often futile way of staving off the onslaught of despair.

OUR GIFTS FROM NATURE

Feelings are bodily reactions that are the healthy built-in technologies for dealing with life's jolts. Our feelings are the healthy devices nature has given us so we can be stirred to resolving problems, creating new solutions, and inventing helpful alternatives. In other words, nature made us feel so we could evolve.

Personal progress does not mean becoming a wooden boy but a real boy. Pinocchio's eyes can water; his veins can pop; his teeth can chatter; his lips can smile. He is not an escapee from life but an arrival in it. We are saddened at loss, angry at injustice, scared by danger, and exuberant in good fortune.

Confronted with any given of life, I may ask, "How can this stretch me?" However, I do this in the context of the feelings that fit the circumstance. For instance, if a loss has occurred, I mourn and feel sadness before I ask about how I can stretch because of it. To meet a given with an immediate concern for how I can learn from my experience or grow from it is jumping the gun. It is a form of no to a full experience.

Yes sounds more like this: "How can I go through this with my eyes wide open? How can I go through this with all my feelings? Then I will be in the best position to grow from the events." This is the yes we were born with. It is unconditioned by age-old platitudes or mental analyses. A yes to feelings is the station stop before we get to philosophical explanations, theological consolations, or encouraging maxims. At that station is our earthiness, our natural passion, and our sanity. In strictly ascetic traditions, the spiritual practices are meant to curb or blunt our natural reactions. That approach is dangerous not only to our health but to our humanness. We evolve by being more human, not less.

Each of the givens of life evokes feelings. To grieve is the appropriate response to loss; it is the form yes takes in the face of loss. It consists of allowing ourselves to feel the full weight of our sadness about an ending, our anger at the loss, and our fear that we will never find a suitable replacement. Any feeling we express fully can connect with other feelings. For example, our sadness can lead us to anger, our anger to fear, and ultimately to the joy of release. The sanguine paradox is that full embrace of feeling leads to letting go: When we gently hold our fear in a hospitable way, we cease holding on to it.

For instance, your husband runs off with your best friend. After a while you get in touch with your anger about the betrayal by both of them. Then, later, you notice a primitive fear arising. You are afraid you will never be free of the grief and obsession about what happened to you. You are afraid you may never find another partner or be able to trust one. You work on yourself in therapy; you forgo all retaliation and practice loving-kindness; you take this book to heart. Gradually you are less obsessed, less sad, less angry, less afraid. You are proud of how you came through it all, and a joyful sense of liberation and a new life open to you. One night, alone and content, you smile as you recall a sentence from *Omoo* by Herman Melville, a book you read in high school and never thought of till now: "By noon, the island had gone down in the horizon; and all before us was the wide Pacific." You muse how this sentence was saved in your memory until you needed it, and you finally see how all the givens of your recent life have been graces.

Many of us have been living for years in our heads or in our defended egos, our makeshift shanties. We do this because we are afraid of our own feelings and of the intimacy they create when others see and share them. Feelings are the fast track to intimacy. They reveal us not as tensed against impact and trenchantly in control but as vulnerable and softened. We become disarming and appealing. Do we avoid feelings because we fear the closeness that may result?

We sometimes know we are feeling something, but it does not state its name. When we give up our refuges of abstraction and intellectualization, we even welcome our unnamable feelings with an unconditional yes. We do this when we let them have their own career in us without interruption. Our bodies know how to do this, since feelings are physical. A healthy body actually becomes an assisting force that makes it easier for us to bear and express our feelings safely and effectively. A body on drugs cannot go through the grief process, for instance; neither can an exhausted or ill-fed body nor one that is trying to look strong.

HOW FEELINGS BECOME SAFE

We will only express our feelings if we feel safe enough to do so. That is a healthy protective mechanism. The work becomes making them safe, avoiding relationships and places where safety is impossible. The four major feelings are in fact SAFE: Sadness, Anger, Fear, and Exuberance. These are the fundamental emotions that underlie much of what we think, say, and do.

Feelings can be appreciated as our built-in technologies for facing the facts of life. Each given evokes one or more of these basic feelings, and to feel something in the face of a given is our way of saying yes. Changes and endings make sadness part of life. Changes and endings are processed and accepted by the experience of sadness. In other words, sadness helps us let go and move on, like all the feelings. We become sad because there is a given of change and ending.

The fact that things do not always go according to plan can arouse anger and also fear, because we realize that threatening events may befall us. The unpredictability of life is handled and worked through by our feelings of anger and fear. This is how we move on instead of being fixated on the "raw deal" we think the universe gave us.

The fact that things are not always fair certainly makes anger appropriate; anger is displeasure about injustice. Anger leads to action to bring about justice, and this helps us move forward in courageous ways. The fact that pain is part of life evokes grief and the search for healing. Without pain we might never go deeply into our feelings and into our inner powers of self-regeneration. And the given that people are not always loyal evokes grief, growth, and forgiveness. What is given is always ultimately a gift.

Life also includes pleasure and fulfillment. This is also a major given, but one that is less likely to cause us any problems. Exuberance arises and is the body's way of saying yes to the joy of life.

We were born with a full potential to experience and express all our feelings. But in order to become activated and ready for use, feelings have to be safe from early life onward. This happens when our feelings are mirrored by our parents in infancy and childhood and when others in the course of life mirror us too. Mirroring means that a feeling is greeted with the five A's: attention, acceptance, appreciation, affection, and allowing. These are the components of caring and understanding. In our early childhood, mirroring was the way a module for each of the four major feelings became safely installed in us so that each could ever after become activated in full-bodied, healthy ways. If the module of a feeling was not installed fully in childhood, its settings in our body-soul-mind may be muted or distorted.

Mirroring in childhood and in adult intimacy make it possible to feel safe enough to cry in sadness, to raise our voice in anger, to quake in fear, or to laugh in joy. In other words, our feelings are legitimated, honored, and welcomed. They are not met with contempt, shame, or threat. They are not inhibited, judged, ridiculed, or punished. We are not told what we should feel, nor are we told we are not feeling what we know we are feeling.

The feelings that were mirrored in childhood are now more easily expressed by us to our partner and accepted from our partner too. Mirroring equips us for intimacy, the giving and receiving of feelings.

In adult life, as in childhood, we feel the need to receive from those we love. There are times when we want to be held or mirrored by others. This need may become neediness as we demand more than others can give. If I am wanting to be held and my partner cannot come through in this moment, there are two steps I can take: First, it is up to me to accept reality: "I cannot get what I want right now." Second, I stay with myself. This means I remain where I am and simply experience the need with no attempt to fill or escape it. I do not rebuke my partner, have a drink, or turn on the TV. I let myself feel what I am feeling without even an attempt to understand it. A marvelous and paradoxical shift may then occur: *My willingness to stay with my own feelings becomes the equivalent of being lovingly held. An unconditional yes to reality enlarges my way of finding fulfillment.*

LOVE LIBERATES

Most people think of love as a feeling, but love is not so much a feeling as a way of being present. Love is a context for the five A's and a commitment to show them. Love is an inner given of goodwill. Saint Thomas Aquinas defines love as "willing good things to happen." Love is the essence of our true and deepest self. This innate state is expressed and becomes real in specific ways and at specific times. Essence is real only in the moments in which it is fulfilled existentially. As the poet W. H. Auden says: "Don't tell me you will love me forever. Tell me you will love me Thursday afternoon at four o'clock!" When our feelings happened safely in childhood and happen now in the context of the love that the five A's create, we find it easy to express them, and we do so without embarrassment or inhibition. We show sadness with tears, grief, and a down mood. We show anger nonviolently but nonetheless strongly. We show fear without shame and without groveling. We show exuberance with abandon.

In addition, we do not use any of our feelings as ploys, charms, maneuvers, or strategies to manipulate others. "Turning on the waterworks" is not in the repertory of a person with self-respect; neither is theatrical intimidation that looks like anger but is abuse. In that instance, we may *exhibit* feelings but not really be expressing them.

All four of the major feelings are positive: they help us unfold as people. No feeling is inherently negative or inappropriate even if it seems unjustified. What is negative is repressing a feeling or being possessed by one. Some feelings are painful, but they become less painful as we allow them to move through us and as we no longer fear them. Shame, self-blame, and impatience with ourselves are the villains that make feelings such as fear and sadness more painful than they need to be.

Most of us have not tried just sitting in and through a feeling experience. We have not trusted ourselves enough to let our feelings take their full course. So we never find out that a feeling is not so tough on us as we imagine it will be. We miss out on how much better we feel when we let go instead of hold back. Nothing is so hard to handle as the fear of facing it.

Feeling itself may be associated with fear and a sense of powerlessness. We fear losing love or approval if we show our emotions. Our fear of upsetting others is the fear that they will not love us if we are true to ourselves. Some of us have been taught to believe that feelings are embarrassing, impolite, or rude. Those judgments come from the world of fear, not from the world of free speech, which is what feelings really are.

Feelings are not bad or wrong, only unpleasant at times. We add a layer of pain to an already unpleasant feeling when we believe it is wrong of us to feel it. We then equate that feeling with guilt. For instance, we do not like feeling jealousy and we make it worse by rebuking ourselves for feeling what is a normal given of any relationship. Perhaps we are embarrassed or afraid of how vulnerable we have become in the relationship.

Feelings can be time machines. They may carry us back to our childhood. We fear abandonment because when it happens, we feel powerless to change it, as we were in childhood. Is adulthood, for some of us, about becoming more and more in control so we will not have to feel that powerlessness ever again? When someone rejects us, we may become so sad as to feel devastated, lonely, and bereft. We may feel then the way we did when our parents turned away from us or when friends in school rejected us. A sense of despair and powerlessness (the same thing really) is a clue to this connection with our past. To come to terms with our feelings is to be vulnerable to the arrows of the past still flying through the skies of the present.

Other people may be catalysts of our feelings, but no one is a cause of them. The experience of a feeling is like rubbing two sticks together. One stick cannot be singled out as the one that caused the fire. Two people or a person and an event have to rub together for the spark of a feeling to result.

HOW FEAR HOLDS US BACK

In infancy and childhood we felt an instinctive need for connection with our caregivers. This need for connection lasts all through our lives. Connection can be shown most deeply by the five A's. There may have been or will be disruptions of our connectedness, but repair is always possible in what D. W. Winnicott calls "an atmosphere of mended failures." Feelings are safe when we are sure that the given of making mistakes will be accepted.

Neurotic fear is the mortal and relentless foe of our lively energy. The counterpart of fear is excitement. To be afraid is to repress our excitement about the challenge we are facing. Instead we make contact only with the danger and our own sense of inadequacy in dealing with it. A practice is to ask ourselves, when we are afraid: "What am I afraid to get excited about?" and then to allow the excitement to come through. Feelings are the way excitement is greeted and permitted.

Sometimes fear feels like an alien presence, a cunning demon that possesses us. This happens when we do not affirm our fear as belonging to us. If fear feels dark, it helps to say, as Prospero did in *The Tempest,* "This thing of darkness I acknowledge [as] mine."

Fear is part of us and is meant to be felt and let go of. What does fear feel like when it possesses us rather than passes through us, as it is meant to do? It batters us in body, heart, and mind. It is ruthless and pervasive, refusing to follow the rules of fair play. Fear knows our Achilles' heel and goes for it every time. It kicks us when we are down. Our mind's defenses are of no avail against this infiltrator that burrows in and won't let go no matter how we fight or plead. Fear compels us to make imprudent choices and then laughs at us for our rashness. It kills our two best friends: trust in ourselves and trust in the possibility of an alternative outcome to the one our catastrophizing mind is crafting.

Our best hopes are guts and grace, the only defenses fear cannot defeat. What are guts in this context? A commitment to the triple-A practice, which requires us to

Admit we are afraid
Allow the feeling of fear to be felt fully
Act so that we are not stopped or driven by fear

How do we acknowledge grace in this context? Begin the practice by asking for assistance from a power higher than ego and end with thanks for the help.

All four of the main feelings are our pathways into our lively energy. Fear as repression—fashionable these days—debits our lively energy. "Keeping our cool" is freezing our aliveness. Some practices in the self-help movement may present a significant drawback when it comes to the expression of feelings in a direct and gritty way. Many of us use therapy, herbs, yoga, and other techniques to blunt our contact with raw feeling. Behind this poignant enterprise may be a need to be in control and a fear of our feelings. We fear feelings because we wonder if we will be able to turn them off when we want to, that is, be in control of them. We fear feelings because they are not pretty sometimes, that is, we are not in control of how they may come out. We fear feelings because they may lead to falling apart, and we cannot handle that possibility as a given for us, so in control all the time. We may fear sadness because we do not want to face the messy task of grieving. When we are grieving, it may seem more courageous to keep a stiff upper lip than to cry openly and vehemently. We talk ourselves out of our grief and lose our connection to the sadness that makes us such touching and appealing beings. The best comfort, ironically, is the result of feeling our sadness fully, noticing we have survived it, and opening to the affection others will feel toward us, with all its resulting closeness. Often when we show our feelings, we are held in them by those who love us or begin to love us in that moment. Is this what we have *feared* for so long?

We may fear others' anger because of its association with violence or danger. The greatest danger may be the sense of a loss of connection with the person who is angry at us: "He is mad, so he will leave me." We may fear expressing our own anger because we do not want to lose the approval of others. We are afraid to say "Ouch!" after being hurt because that may sever our connection to another person. When we are aroused to anger, it may seem that it is more mature to "talk it out" than to show the feeling. Behind our fear of anger is a fear of asserting ourselves and of showing our vulnerability to others' behavior. Fear of anger prevents us from displaying our deepest needs, values, wishes, and potentials, the ingredients of our true self, the steps to evolution. How can intimacy or destiny unfold when the best of us has to be hidden?

Worst of all, we also fear fear itself. When we are afraid, it may seem that it is more adult to cover up rather than to display our sense of powerlessness. We are afraid we might lose control. We are ashamed to be seen as afraid. We confuse fear with cowardice or inadequacy. The fear of fear can lead to our taking so many precautions that we never get to live the life we want to live. We walk on eggshells instead of bursting out of the egg.

We may fear exuberance. We may distrust joy and spontaneity. We are afraid that we may look foolish if we suddenly dance. We may believe in the superstition that laughter leads to tears. When we are exuberant, it may seem that it is more mature to keep our cool than to show the all-out excitement we feel. We are afraid to lose control, afraid of our animal nature.

The freedom to feel leads to fearless honesty: we can stop working the angles. We can be who we are. We can act spontaneously and freely express our emotions. Gradually we notice that we like what we spontaneously say and do, that we are proud of our honesty, that we are no longer trying to look good. We are saying yes to ourselves as we are. This is precisely how our basic goodness is revealed.

> *The goodness in human nature is in its suitability and aptitude for grace and that goodness can never be lost, not even by sin.*
>
> —Saint Thomas Aquinas

THE LIFE SPAN OF A FEELING

Fear of feelings bottlenecks us. We fear that a feeling may possess us and never calm down. Actually, a feeling wants to be over and done with. Feelings, like everything else in life, are ever-changing and impermanent. Like attraction and repulsion, feelings flow over a bell-shaped curve. We do not have to fear being permanently angry if we show anger. Once we let the cycle begin, it keeps flowing to a resolution and repose. All we have to do is merge with it. To say "He holds on to his anger" is not accurate. One cannot hold on to an angry feeling, only to the judgments, wishes for retaliation, blame, and other mind-sets that we attach to it.

This is how the cycle of a complete feeling experience flows through us:

A stimulus ——➤ arousal of a feeling ——➤ showing the feeling ——➤ cooling down ——➤ a calm openness to what may come next as we get on with life ——➤ readiness for the next stimulus and beginning again.

The variance and movement of a feeling shows us why we use the word *emotion*. That word literally means "move out." True feelings or emotions move us and we move through them. True mental health, like the evolution of the universe, is a continually adaptive and flowing process. Feelings show the same motion.

A mindful yes to our feelings means that we simply allow them to happen and notice ourselves feeling them. We do not fall prey to the dangers of attachment or aversion. Real feelings help us do this work because they want to come and they want to go. We may interrupt ourselves at any point during this natural sequence, preferring an incomplete experience. For instance:

• We may prevent ourselves from noticing the trigger-point stimulus by engaging in denial or dissociation.
• We may interrupt the arousal of a feeling by intellectualizing what happened or explaining it away or excusing it or failing even to notice it.

• We may interrupt the expression of the feeling by simply stuffing it or by going so out of control that it is no longer a feeling but drama.

• We may interrupt the cooldown and the going on by holding on to a smoldering resentment (based on the Latin for "to feel again"), which becomes stress rather than resolution. "She is always afraid" may mean "She has not yet expressed her real fear." We may be refusing to face what may next come sailing over the horizon.

At any of these points we may turn to alcohol, drugs, food, or addiction as ways of stunting the life cycle of our feelings.

Here is an example of the process when we allow a feeling fully: Someone hurts us purposely. That is the stimulus. We are aroused to anger and feel hurt, a form of sadness. We show our anger without spite and our sadness without shame. We notice the feelings diminishing, and soon we get on with our lives. We do all this irrespective of how the other person reacts and with no attempt to make him or her wrong or to retaliate against the person. That is loving-kindness.

It's important to note that rarely does only one feeling arise in us at a time. Feelings are notes, and they join in complex chords. For instance, sadness almost always accompanies anger and vice versa, since in both instances there is grief involved. We are sad because of a loss of some kind. We are displeased and angry because of the loss attendant upon a perceived injustice.

Some feelings, for example, those associated with grief about a heavy loss, may never lead to full resolution. There is a note of inconsolability in some grief no matter how much we cry or how mirrored we may be by those who care about us. We can say yes to the given that some of our experiences remain unresolved and unfinished. This is not because we are inadequate but because reality is sometimes just that stubborn—another part of the mystery of life. There are some aches that never fully abate. Perhaps this is what Virgil meant by "the tears in things." Perhaps this is what the Buddha meant by the first noble truth, the universality and ineradicability of dissatisfaction.

A spiritually aware person loves going with the flow of feelingful events. The old advice for safety during an earthquake was to sit in a doorway with your back firmly against one side and your feet tensed against the other. But this is essentially fighting against what wants to happen—the new advice is to roll into a ball and flow with it.

The natural cycle of an emotion also helps us see more clearly why love is not really a feeling. Love, unlike the four feelings, is not something we move through. It is an ongoing context and commitment that is shown in here-and-now choices. The showing of love is time-bound and transitory, but love itself is enduring and reliable. Acts of love are existential, but love itself is essential, beyond the ravages of cycles or the perils of loss.

HOW DO WE RECEIVE THE FEELINGS OF OTHERS?

In order to fully receive others' feelings and help them to move through their emotions, we stay present with the five A's and without the mind-sets of ego: fear, attachment, control, judgment, complaint, blame, contempt, or censure. Here are examples:

• We let others experience grief in their own way, with respect for the time it takes them, with compassion for their pain, and without trying to fix them.
• We listen to their anger with rapt attention and without ego defenses or any attempt to prove they are wrong or to retaliate.
• We stay present with them as companions in their fear.
• We encourage and join in their fun and joy, saying: "Go for it."

Intimacy then comes to mean the exchange of our feelings *with* the support shown in the five A's and *without* interfering mind-sets. An adult relationship that has made even one of the four feelings verboten does not allow the full monty of intimacy.

Most of us do not fully show or fully receive feelings. It might have been dangerous to express feelings in childhood. We may have been forbidden from or ridiculed for having them. For instance, a parent who could not handle our tears may have made fun of us or tried to tell us we had "nothing to cry about." Now we may try to keep a "stiff upper lip" so our real griefs are not expressed or even guessed.

What do we do when a friend is suffering? Do we immediately try to comfort her by showing the ultimate meaning in it all? Or do we agree that her pain is meaningless if she sees it that way? Any words at all may impinge upon the other's experience. The appropriate etiquette is simply to *stay*. Friendship shown in this way is a spiritual practice of mindfulness. We stay with no judgment or advice or words of comfort. This is how a compassionate yes is expressed in response to the anguish of others. To stay with another's feelings with no attempt to change, fix, or reduce them honors connectedness.

Romeo says to Juliet in the tomb: "I still will stay with thee." His love takes the form of staying. What Friar Lawrence says to Juliet is "I dare no longer stay." His love has been overridden by fear. In the Bhagavad Gita, a core sacred text of Hinduism, the god Krishna appears to Arjuna, a human who is facing a battle. Krishna promises to stay with Arjuna throughout his trial and does. Christ says: "Behold, I stay with you always." Buddha, smiling at us, seems to make the same promise. Staying is how love is made present. It does not erase reality for us, only accompanies us through it. To stay with our own reality is to become divinely loving of ourselves.

TRACKING OUR FEELINGS

Give sorrow words. The grief that does not speak
Whispers the oe'rfraught heart and bids it break.
—WILLIAM SHAKESPEARE, *Macbeth*

The first challenge in expressing our feelings is to take personal responsibility for what we feel, since our feeling response is subjective, based on our unique beliefs and needs. An action does not lead to a feeling unless a belief intervenes. It is as simple as ABC: *Action* or stimulus leads to *belief* about its meaning, which leads to *consequent* feeling. We are, as adults, always reexamining our beliefs in case they need upgrading. For instance, I am jealous because my partner has what seems like an intimate bond with someone at work. This is a stimulus. Their friendship feels threatening and scary to me. But where did the fear come from? My belief is that someone is taking my place. My fear is based on that belief, not on their relationship.

The second challenge is to show our feelings in ways that do not threaten or impinge on others' freedom. For instance, sometimes when we feel distressed, we might call a friend and try to get her to feel distressed too. Healthy people share their feelings to be mirrored by others, not to unload their feelings onto others. Adults seek feedback on how to handle their feelings; they don't make others carry them. And they ask for compassion, not to induce pity or to get others to take retaliatory action, but as a way of garnering support.

The third challenge is to maintain a connection with others no matter what we may feel toward them: "I am angry at you and still love you. My commitment to you is not lessened by the anger I feel now." Authentic feelings do not have to become disruptions of our closeness to one another. They can be communications that lead to deeper communion.

A useful practice for the recovery of our right to our feelings is to track what happens. How does each emotion arise? What happens when we feel it coming on? How do we show it or not show it? Where did this style come from? These questions move in both directions, exploring both our feelings toward others and our reactions to others' feelings toward us. Notice how the tracking of each feeling may be directly linked to the model our parents gave us or to long-held inhibitions.

For example, I have noticed that whenever someone seems to be getting angry and upset with me, I use all my powers of persuasion to calm that person down. I smile, talk reasonably, and try to smooth things over. I convince myself that this is in keeping with my commitment to nonviolence. But ultimately I can't be fooled. I know this placating style has fear behind it. I see a connection to my childhood, when anger was expressed in abusive, violent ways, and so I became frightened by rage. My powerlessness in childhood now makes me afraid of healthy anger. Yet I am learning that as an adult I can trust myself to handle abuse by stopping it midstream or exiting the situation. I do not have to be powerless anymore, and I can now allow anger to arise in others and in me with less fear and more self-confidence. The triple-A technique—admit fear, allow feeling, act—mentioned earlier in this chapter has helped me a lot and so has the practice of loving-kindness.

There is one caveat in expressing feelings, and it has to do with trust. If we cannot trust that the person we're speaking to can receive our feelings with the respect that is shown by the five A's and without a plan to use our feelings against us later, it is better not to express them in the moment. We can share our feelings later with someone who can be trusted. Indeed, when a feeling arises, we require more connection than usual. This is why we feel so vulnerable when we show feelings and why we may be afraid to do so. As Shakespeare says: "I have said too much unto a heart of stone."

It is a given that some people will show us the five A's. It is also a given that sometimes people will not pay attention to us, not accept us, not appreciate us, not feel or show affection toward us, and some people will try to control us rather than honor our freedom. If we can be flexible and resilient in our relationships, we will notice what is missing, feel sad about it, and not have to retaliate. These three responses constitute a spiritual practice of yes to how others are, without protest or blame. We will then let go of an arrogant entitlement to the five A's, appreciate them when they come our way, and grow in compassion for those who can't easily love.

WHAT FEELINGS ARE NOT

Our feelings are our truth. To hide them in ourselves or run from them in others is to fail to face the truth that sets us free and the contact that makes us coherent to—and vulnerable to—one another. Moreover, a substitution of feelings does not work. Truth in feelings means honoring the feeling that is appropriate to our experience. No matter how much we rage, we can never be satisfied if we really want to cry.

Feelings are not beliefs, needs, sensations, emotional states, or judgments. We use the one word *feel* to cover many subtle possibilities in human communication.

This statement:	*Really means:*
• I feel he is the best candidate.	• I believe he is the best candidate.
• I feel like being held.	• I need to be held.
• That touch feels good.	• That touch brings pleasant sensations.
• I feel lonely.	• When I am lonely I feel . . .
• I feel you betrayed me.	• I judge you for your behavior, *or* when I am betrayed I feel . . . , *or* I believe you betrayed me.

Language helps us find our real feelings. Simple words such as *sad, mad, scared, glad* tend to denote bedrock feelings. However, there are many more obviously Latin- or French-based words that seem to represent feelings but in fact do not. For instance, the following words appear to denote feelings but are actually judgments about how others have treated us: *betrayed, abandoned, rejected, disappointed, humiliated,* or *isolated*. Each of these is a belief that activates certain story lines and subtly blames or implicates another person in our distress. Each is meant to point a finger at someone who dared to do our ego wrong.

It is an adult project to seek out the true feeling that hides behind the belief. For example, "I am sad because of how disappointed I am." This shifts the focus from how we have been treated to how we can show our authentic feelings and thereby take responsibility for them. Healing begins and proceeds with attention to what is real, that is, to mindful focus and the release of what we feel.

We may also confuse feelings with states of mind like loneliness or jealousy. We do better to acknowledge the authentic feelings behind our inner states. Instead of "I feel lonely," try "When I am lonely, I feel . . ." This may station us in one or more of the four basic feelings rather than make us head for food, alcohol, drugs, sex, or shopping.

Jealousy is, in fact, not a feeling but a combination of three feelings: anger, fear, and sadness—with paranoid fantasies obsessively embroidering them. To identify our real feelings is a way of taking responsibility for our predicament rather than distracting ourselves with getting back at others or turning to addictions for comfort. "Now that I am jealous, I feel . . ."

There are many other examples of feelings being confused with states of mind. "I feel hostile" is really "I am angry." "I am uncomfortable" may be "I am scared." "I feel good" may be "I am joyful." It is a good practice to go to our acronym SAFE (sadness, anger, fear, exuberance) and check in with ourselves to see which one or more feelings are really at play. Since the first part of psychological work is articulating our own truth, we are better off knowing what we are really feeling so we can decode and resolve our experience accurately.

Hate can be confused with anger. Hate has five traits: strong anger, a malicious need to hurt the other, an insatiable craving for revenge, an inability to forgive no matter how penitent the other may be, and giving up on the other. Hate is a defense against our anger, grief, and powerlessness. We cannot stand those feelings, so we project them onto others as hate. It is a dangerous and frustrating enterprise that evolved people have left behind.

Does this mean that there is no righteous anger? The difference between anger and hate is that anger seeks to remove an injustice. Hate seeks rather to destroy the unjust. Anger engages someone. Hate distances. Anger is expressed and let go of. Hate can never be satisfied or completed but abides as resentment. In that sense, hate is an impotent rage. Hate is to the dark side of an individual what war is to the dark side of the collective. Despair is the origin of hate, since the one hating has given up on the other. Despair is the origin of war, since one or both sides have given up on peaceful solutions.

Raw feelings, like anger, come from the limbic—emotional—system of the brain. Hostility or envy masquerade as feelings. Actually, they contain feelings but are mainly social displays. These come from more sophisticated brain centers. Thus even by brain location and origin, feelings differ from judgments, beliefs, or socially manipula-tive exhibitions. The real feelings remain: sadness, anger, fear, and gladness. But complex beings like us love complexity.

Most of us have noticed in ourselves and in others that one feeling tends to dominate in our personality. It is our favorite resort, our de-fault setting. For instance, some people cry when anything big hap-pens; some get angry at the drop of a hat; some automatically find something to be worried about; and some laugh things off easily. In my workshops, I sometimes ask for a show of hands from the audi-ence about which feeling they feel most in their daily lives. Invariably, fear is the most frequent choice by a margin of about seven to one.

FEELINGS ARE THREE-DIMENSIONAL

Feelings resonate in our bodies with changes in heartbeat, pulse, breathing; release of serotonin, adrenaline, norepinephrine; constric-tion or expansion of blood vessels; muscle tightening; changes in tem-perature; and more. Feelings also have psychological and spiritual dimensions. In a healthy expression of feelings all three dimensions—body, mind, soul—are honored.

To show feelings with physical gestures and full bodily resonance helps us be true to the visceral nature of our experience. Society may frown on this kind of full, or even florid, expression of feeling, but the challenge of personal freedom is to design our behavior in accord with what is earthy and natural.

We are rational *animals* and yet we live mostly in our heads. Feel-ings help us grant hospitality to our instinctive, passionate, primal in-clinations. They open the door so we can take more risks, be more defiant of the status quo, more daring in our imagination and behav-ior. To be rational is to be in control and this may be why we feel safer in that realm and deny our citizenship in the animal kingdom. Feel-ings, along with dancing, shouting, joking, and other ventures out-side the box, release our fuller nature.

At the same time, psychologically, feelings are meant to be ad-dressed, processed, and resolved. When we commit ourselves to doing this, we are no longer living an unexamined life. We are choosing consciousness, and that is a choice for evolution—our life purpose and our most exciting goal. This builds our self-esteem.

The spiritual dimension of feelings comes through when we are thankful for the lively energy our feelings arouse. We also sense an identity between our personal energy and the energy in the collective life of the universe. Then we realize, joyfully, that our uniquely felt aliveness is the very same power that combusts the distant stars and rolls the wild waves.

May I find safety in my feelings, and may those I come in contact with find feeling responses in me so that love can flourish between us and in all the universe.

NINE

A YES TO WHO I AM

THE GIVENS are predicaments we will be facing again and again in life. We can take them as information rather than as provocations. Such a serene yes helps us grow. Then the conditions of our existence can lead to psychological growth, spiritual maturation, and mystical consciousness. Paradoxically, an unconditional yes to who I am, how others are, and what the world is places me in the best position to grow. We can say yes to participating in our own evolution and working toward our life purpose in three ways: by cultivating psychological health, spiritual maturity, and mystical oneness or spiritual awakening. These are not three levels that follow one another linearly; they stand as one integral whole. Each is complete only when it includes the other two. To integrate these three dimensions of ourselves is to combine sanity and sanctity.

More and more in the self-help movement, we are realizing that a truly healthy person is someone who is virtuous too. For instance, to have self-esteem is a psychological accomplishment. But without humility, a virtue that results from spiritual practice, it is simply decorative and not authentically and deeply instilled. Psychological work does not motivate us toward loving-kindness, toward a refusal to retaliate, or even toward integrity in our business dealings. For those virtues we need a spiritual consciousness that complements our psychological work.

On the other hand, spiritual practice does not help us process, grieve, and heal our childhood issues. For example, we can sit in meditation regularly and practice mindfulness, but we may still resent our parents for neglect or abuse, or even worse, act out on others as our parents acted toward us. A spiritually aware person is one who has learned to acknowledge and work with his or her unresolved issues, dark side, and inflated ego. Meditation is not sufficient to deal with all of this. Psychological tools provide state-of-the-art—and necessary—help.

Indeed, such integration assists us so much in the fulfillment of our life purpose: the enlightened moment of letting light through so that everyone can experience love through us. An unconditional and mindful yes to what is arouses us to activate and expand our threefold potential: personal, spiritual, and transpersonal. Thus, a whole person is one who works on psychological issues, engages in spiritual practice, and is imbued with a sense of oneness with the universe.

PSYCHOLOGICALLY

To say yes to our personal psychological development is to engage in the work it takes to build a healthier ego, that is, a healthier way of functioning in the world.

If we have not succumbed to a life of hate, despair, or spite, we have survived the buffets of childhood and adulthood quite victoriously so far. Psychological health is a combination of thought and action in the world that keeps us evolving. It is, first of all, the key to a self-esteem that brings both serenity and happiness. Second, psychological health means effective relationships in which it becomes possible to love without fear. As part of your own personal work, use this as a checklist to track your progress toward psychological health:

• Assertiveness in our dealings with others so that we express our deepest needs, values, and wishes without inhibition and with respect for others

• Making peace with childhood issues so that they no longer strongly control our present life or direct our style of relating to others

• A program for dealing with fear, guilt, anger, and addiction so that we are not driven or stopped by any of them

• A recognition that our ego can become inflated or self-centered and a choice not to be ruled by those distortions

• A reliable inner program, to which we are committed for handling needs, conflicts, suffering, losses, challenges, and decision making

• A commitment to address, process, and resolve issues that arise in us and between us and others

• An awareness that people—and we—have a dark shadow side and a program to deal with it creatively, including making amends when we are at fault

• A recognition that our strong reactions to others, either of aversion or of attraction, may be projections based on our own shadow, our ego, or our early life issues

• An evolving sense of self-respect and respect for others with all their diverse virtues and vices

• An ability to maintain personal boundaries and yet be authentic in our relationships with others

• The ability to be intimate without being stopped by fear or pushed by compulsion

• An ever-evolving and trustworthy intuitive sense and a nondefensive attention to the feedback of others

• The twofold ability to engage animatedly with new people entering our lives and to let go serenely of those who are leaving

• A recognition that these qualities may require the aid of therapy, self-help books, classes, or twelve-step programs and a willingness to go to those resources.

SPIRITUALLY

Psychological work and spiritual practice are not two separate tasks but one simultaneous project of human becoming. In psychological health, our purpose is to fulfill our life goals, find personal happiness, and enjoy effective relationships with those around us. In spiritual practice we expand our purpose so that our motivation includes the happiness and evolution of the whole world. This is not a totally different realm of human experience. It is, rather, a deepening of our sense of aliveness, which makes for a more loving presence in the world. Spiritual practices are the skillful means to this deepening. They may include meditation, loving-kindness, religious devotion, and virtuous living.

Evolution makes it clear that something is built into the nature of things that wants survival to take precedence over destruction and wants love to conquer hate. As Gandhi said: "Our experience is that human beings live on. From this I infer that it is the law of love that rules mankind. It gives me ineffable joy to go on trying to prove that." When we affirm such a purpose and cooperate with it, love blooms and war and hostility cease to destroy our world. The project of becoming human turns out to be the same project as nature's: continual transcendence. As the scholar of religion Mircea Eliade says: "Nature expresses something that transcends us." What is transcended? Our self-centered ego driven by fear and greed.

What are our commitments as we become more spiritually evolved persons? (Use this list to explore the effects of your spiritual practices on your present lifestyle.)

• To act virtuously in all our dealings with others, with no motivation to take advantage or gain adulation
• To show compassion and love not only to those we care about but to all beings
• To befriend and transform the shadow in ourselves and others so that it yields spiritual riches

- To care that others find the spiritual gifts we have discovered and to do all we can to share them, especially by example
- To let our life become the story not only of our own advancement but also of our cooperation with the evolution of our planet: a sense of universal purpose and service
- To be free of the constraints of ego, that is, no longer to be driven or stopped by fear, attachment, control, or arrogant entitlement
- To give up all forms, however subtle, of retaliation or violence so that we replace anger with activism and our paranoia with purpose
- To honor the freedom of others and to work for justice in the world through nonviolence
- To form a coherent foundation or framework of values and standards from which our life choices are made
- To trust more and more that the world and all that happens in it have a larger meaning and purpose than that of gratifying our ego
- To trust an abiding sense that something, we know not what, we know not how, is always at work to bring us and all beings to our highest capacity for love
- To be thankful when some of our steps become shifts into higher consciousness
- To act with humility and virtuous standards
- To remain aware that, ultimately, we do not achieve spiritual wisdom but receive it as a grace—and it is always and everywhere available
- To trust more and more that the world and all that happens in it has a larger meaning and purpose than that of gratifying our ego. Yes makes this happen, as Dag Hammarskjöld said: "At some moment I did answer Yes to Someone—or Something—and from that hour I was certain that existence is meaningful and that, therefore, my life, in self-surrender, had a goal."

Is my heart grand enough to accommodate all the powers that want to find me and work through me?

MYSTICALLY

Consciousness is how we connect to the world around us. Mystical experience is pure content-free consciousness. *Mystical* here does not mean occult or esoteric or parapsychological. It refers to the possibility of equating our own consciousness with universal consciousness: The personal is the natural is the transpersonal. Jan van Ruysbroeck, a protégé of Meister Eckhart's, wrote: "The mystic goes both up and down the ladder of contemplation. His contact with the divine must evoke the complementary impulse of charity to all the world."

A mystic finds and walks a spiritual path without the need for mediators—even without the need for a path. A mystic has gone beyond forms and divisions into pure unity. She or he has an intuitive discernment that transcends and defies rational thought. Religion and spiritual practices offer a context for awakening, but mysticism is the fulfillment of awakening.

When we grasp ourselves with mystical vision, our human nature, like nature itself, is radiating everywhere in the universe. This means there is no division between inside and outside, inner and outer, surface and depth, body and soul. These are all provisional distinctions we employ to distinguish—for convenience—the individual thinking ego mind from a boundless single energy animating all the universe. In each tradition the words may differ, but the experience is the same. Buddha nature approximates what is called Christ consciousness in Christianity, the breath of God in Judaism, and higher consciousness or the life force in humanism. The archetypal Self described by Jung is related to these concepts as well. Mystics have discovered a larger life that is at once our origin and our goal, "the center of which is everywhere and the circumference nowhere," as the German theologian Nicholas of Cusa described God. God as transcendent may be a way of affirming that our highest value is in the transcendent rather than the limited.

Through spiritual practice we keep progressing. In mystical union the entire pageant of evolution is happening in this enlightened moment, always and already, here and now. This is no longer growth but perfection. Mystical union is a state of grace that is unconjured by work or practice, though it usually follows upon them. Following are some of the qualities the mystical state may include. As a spiritual practice, look for the implications of each item in your present life.

• A recognition that individual consciousness and ego are only provisional designations and repeated suggestions of separate identity and that actually we are interconnected with all that is

• An awareness that everything is permanent because of its cycles of change and renewal and impermanent in its individually enduring identity

• An end to being driven or stopped by fear so that we can be re-leased from the ego's war-strafed world

• An engaged and active compassion for those who are still caught in ego—without feeling that we are superior to them

• A release of unconditional love, intuitive wisdom, and healing power in all we say and do

• A vision of the world as an ever-renewing celebration in which is played out the mystical marriage of apparent opposites

• A vision of nature as the container, preserver, and developer of consciousness

• A contribution to the liberation of the collective human shadow through personal moral integrity and commitment to the welfare of others, as in the bodhisattva vows

• A recognition that all is grace and synchronicity, so that, no mat-ter how chaotic or puzzling life becomes, our destiny is being beauti-fully fulfilled

• A sense of a transcendent life behind all finite appearances, a pervasive nonduality underlying all that is

• An awareness that the divine is the deepest reality of the human and the natural and not a separate state or a separate being, except in personification and metaphor

• An abiding and unshakable loving-kindness toward ourselves and others

- An awareness that everything on this list is inadequate and imprecise, since words cannot contain—or even successfully approximate—the mystery of the infinite. As Emily Dickinson says, "Too bright for our infirm Delight / The Truth's superb surprise."

SELF OR NO-SELF?

Form and emptiness are terms often used in Buddhism. A human being has a form that is physical and mental, both unique. In addition, a person is emptiness, buddha mind, big mind, the essential being shared by all humans as well as nature. We might say that form and emptiness are meant to become axis powers so that we can evolve.

We are sometimes confused by the seeming contradiction of our psychological goal to be someone and our spiritual destiny to let go of ego and be no one. It is not an "either . . . or" choice between self and no-self; we are both a conventional self *and* a no-self. We are at once some specific and unique person psychologically (form) and not separate spiritually (emptiness). No-self is not zero but innumerality.

To be a self psychologically means operating from a coherent sense of who we are as we think and act in the world. In a sense, the psychological self is simply a description of a set of operations that keep us afloat in the conventional world. It is a provisional and utilitarian designation, not an ontological reality.

To acknowledge the fact of no self is to let go of the illusion that such a self or ego is permanent, independent, fixed, or solid. The sense of fixity and separation is an impression, not an empirical fact. A realization of our inherent emptiness is an achievement of wisdom. The no-self of Buddhism and mysticism refers to the fact that we are all interrelated and contingent, an interactive system, not a collection of freestanding individuals. When we put the implications of this insight into practice, we act with compassion. Then what we call our identity is seen for what it is: a futile attempt to stay in control.

Our universal connectedness explains our sense of oneness with nature and with others. When we wake up to our true nature, our true interconnectedness, we find that wisdom leads to compassion and we are liberated from the chill and heavy chains of the self-centered ego. No-self is the united reality and harmony of nature that moves us and the other stars.

The fact that there is no separate self does not simply mean that all beings are interconnected with one another. It also means that our conventional identity is a process, not an established structure. Our identity, in other words, is an evolving phenomenon. It is impermanent not only because it is contingent but also because it is continually changing to become what it will never fully be. We will always be more and never final.

The rugged individualism and accent on personal freedom that arose during the romantic movement of the eighteenth century have led directly to the alienation we feel in today's world. We are social animals trying to be separatists. Spirituality has an answer: compassion flowing from a sense of interconnectedness. We begin life as a part, a piece of our mother's body. At birth we begin to individuate. We then establish our own density on the planet by our personality characteristics, our unique desires, our possessions, our relationships, and our accomplishments. These were meant to be the means by which we fulfill ourselves; instead, they sometimes become ends that perpetuate our separateness.

Marie-Louise von Franz, a Jungian analyst, wrote of the Self and the no-self in these words: "The Self is the most individual core of the most individual person and simultaneously the human Self, that is, the Self of all humanity." A Self that is entirely present in all that is can be identified ultimately as the life force. That force, the same in us as in all of nature, does not survive in the every-man-for-himself world, only in the every-person-for-everyone ecological world. The Self is the life force of the universe articulated in this self—yours and mine—here and now.

Our identity is oneness, and our destiny is to act in accord with that oneness. So life happens and thrives, it seems, because of love. Our spiritual destiny is to love as many beings as there are, for as long as we live, in our own unique way, to our full capacity. The more we affirm that others matter as much as we do, the more we find our personal path and our purpose in life. This interconnectedness is how universal evolutionary, that is, ever-ripening, yearnings fulfill themselves in individual lives.

At the same time, kinship with all and the sense of oceanic oneness are suspect when they become ways of beguiling ourselves away from the fact of our own death, the most terrifying implication of the first and most implacable given—that everything changes and ends. Once our spiritual focus is on the unconditional yes to the givens of life, we see through the promises that may be ploys for avoiding confrontation with our own mortality, no matter how mystically charged.

Our yes is to self. This is the equivalent of yes to doing our psychological and spiritual work to become the stable and healthy self we were meant to be. Our yes is to no-self. This is yes to universal compassion that is nonetheless mortal. Our yes is to the higher Self. This is thanks for grace.

> All the lotus lands and all the Buddhas are revealed in my own being.
>
> —*Avatamsaka Sutra*

A STABLE SENSE OF MYSELF

Our sense of self flourishes in an atmosphere that attunes to our feelings by granting us the five A's of attention, acceptance, appreciation, affection, and allowing. Who we are is personally devised, but it is also continually being codetermined by how others act toward us and feel about us. Our self-esteem lies in our satisfaction with our personal competence, yet it also lies in how responsive others are to us, whether they consider us deserving of their love and attentiveness, whether they find us to be worthy of caring about. This is another indicator of the fact of our profound connectedness.

But what exactly defines a coherent, healthy sense of self? Below are the key elements, which can each also be taken on as a set of practices or aspirations we can employ to gain a stronger sense of self.

A Sense of Continuity

I am part of a history. Personally, I am connected to a family and forebears. I have inherited genes from them, and certain talents too. In addition, I am part of the history of humanity. I have a relationship to the collective. I am heir to all the dark and light that humans have brought into the world. The archetypes that drive me are the ones that all humans share. Finally, I am part of nature. I breathe the way other beings do, and I continually exchange air and energy from all beings in the universe. I am what the stars are. My breath is that of the rose and of you.

An Ability to Deal with Problems and People

I accept the good and the bad in life events. I accept the good and the bad in others and in myself. This is how I maintain a sense of self that has stability and constancy. I can love others when they hurt me rather than jump to revenge. The habitual style of ego will kick in with a plan of attack. The work is not to act on that. I become a coherent self when I no longer act on primitive ego reactions. For instance, a driver cuts me off in traffic and I want to get back at him or her. I notice my reaction mindfully and instruct my ego not to get the better of me but to relax. I do not engage in road rage but lift my foot from the accelerator and let the speeding car move on as I make a kindly remark and wish for the driver's safety. When I do these practices of mindfulness and loving-kindness, I become more than an entitled ego, and I like myself a lot more too.

I have powers of self-nurturance. When things become difficult, I can soothe myself. I can fall apart, and I also have ways of reconstituting myself. I fully allow a collapse and then get up. I am not devastated by crises. I have resources lined up to help me get through things.

In the face of pain, I do not avoid or escape but go through it and move on. I can deal with trauma, and if it is too big for me, I can seek help from supportive others or in therapy.

I address, process, and resolve what comes up for me. This means that the events of my life are not just experienced unconsciously but are examined and contemplated with consciousness and a plan for improvement. I do not go through things; I come through them.

I make sense of what happens to me and learn from it. I see all that happens to me in an evolutionary context, that is, as challenges on the heroic journey to self-actualization.

I know what I can and cannot do no matter how many little engines that could have been paraded before me. I know my limits and I accept them as givens. This is how my humility works to lead me to the unconditional and unabashed yes to my uninflated self. With this knowledge I can exercise caution about what I get myself into. I do not go where I know I will be hurt, frightened, or fragmented.

A Responsiveness to Support

People, partners, and parents are not available all the time, so it is important for me to have the skill to look elsewhere for need fulfillment sometimes. I do this without blame, since I have no expectation that any one person could fulfill all my needs all the time. Indeed, more and more I drop such expectations, since they are adverse to an unconditional yes.

I am appreciative and receptive to mirroring from others and I can rely on the holding environment around me. This reliance does not mean that I do not know that sometimes people do not come through, but it does mean I can trust other people. I can receive support and cherish my sense of belonging to a family, a relationship, a community. Now I see that a sense of belonging matters, because I notice that the whole universe thrives on interconnectedness.

"May those who find themselves in a trackless and fearsome wilderness . . . be guarded by beneficent heavenly beings," says Shantideva, an eighth-century Buddhist monk. On the archetypal level, I also have a sense of being upheld by powers that are greater than my own ego or that of others. I am more than my story and I have something to fall back on: a larger life than ego can account for. This is what the psalmist meant by "I will fear no evil, for thou art with me." (Ps. 23:4) The larger divine life does not have to be a personal God, but it does endorse the sense of unity I have with saints and bodhisattvas who have gone before me.

Once I acknowledge God as a personification of an intrapsychic reality, I am no longer so alone in the universe. There is no separate God, as there is no separate human or separate oak tree. I live in a communion of saints and nature. To say that I have nothing at all to fall back on when things go wrong does not accommodate the vast tradition of human spirituality. As I have explained, in the Buddhist tradition, the bodhisattva stays with me till I am enlightened and assures me I am thereby indeed "guarded." The spiritual realization of no-thing is, after all, not nothing. It is rather the realization of there being no reality to separateness. Self-sufficiency contradicts the spiritual principle of the no-self and of interrelatedness.

Adult spirituality does not mean I am on my own; it means I am never on my own. I feel this in nature, which strongly engenders a sense of myself as interconnected.

A Virtuous Framework for Conscious Living

A sense of self includes living life within a framework, that is, within a set of ethics and standards out of which one makes one's choices. This is a helpful guardrail, not a roadblock. It includes a worldview, a way of understanding life. An example is following the moral recommendations of a particular religion or a well-defined philosophy of life (assuming this religious or philosophical system is geared for adults, as described in chapter 6). With such a framework I can place whatever occurs in the world and in myself into a meaningful context. When I meet up with one of the inexorable givens of life, I am no longer thrown for a loop. Whatever happens becomes intelligible as a condition of existence, one that can grant more depth, more compassion, more character as long as I accept it with the unconditional yes of spiritual consciousness.

Living according to a reliable set of ideals, values, goals, and aspirations helps us establish a healthy sense of self that is fulfilled by becoming a more virtuous person. Virtues are the givens of our lives and behavior when we act with integrity and love. Virtues are habits of wholesomeness. They are the actions that emerge from our inner values. Our virtuous actions demonstrate our basic goodness. They are the building blocks of self-respect, character, and integrity. Virtues are inborn gifts for some of us, but all of us can become virtuous by practice. In Hebrew the word for virtue, *ma'alot,* also means steps. We can keep taking the steps, however small, that lead toward virtue. Interior shifts follow, and we are acting virtuously without having to think or plan it, that is, they become givens of our lives. The steps are efforts; the shifts are graces. This is how the divine plan of loving-kindness is fulfilled in us. Our destiny is to display in time a design beyond time.

Theologian Paul Wadell wrote, "To be human is to be born into the world with something to achieve, namely, the fullness of one's human nature, and it is through the virtues that one does so. . . . The virtues are the only guarantee against a wasted life."

Most of us think of virtues in terms of specific words (such as *honesty* and *patience*) rather than in sentences that describe behaviors. However, a spiritual practice of building virtues focuses on them as specific affirmations and actions. Ponder one virtue from the following list each day and look for ways to put it into practice.

• I say yes unconditionally to the givens of human life: Everything will change and end; things will not always go according to my plans; life will not always be fair or pain-free; and people will not always be loving, honest, generous, or loyal.

• I am happy to appear as I am, without pretense and no matter how unflattering. I am not perfect, but I am deeply committed to working on myself. I am noticing that the more I engage in my personal work, the more I care about the world and the part I am privileged to play in its cocreation. Rather than simply pass through experiences without awareness, I choose to pause long enough to address and process what is happening to me. I learn from my own reactions: Tears at a movie invite me to look at my personal griefs. Attraction and repulsion invite me to look at my hidden needs and motives. Memories and images that tug at me invite me to stay with them and to follow their lead into my own unopened spaces.

- I am not caught up in regret or self-reproach because of my mistakes in life. I take it all as a learning experience so I can do better in the future. I make amends whenever I can. And, of course, my mistakes become a valuable passport to humility.

- I examine my conscience regularly. I do a searching inventory not only about how I have hurt others but about how I may not have activated or shared my gifts, how I may still be holding on to prejudices or the will to retaliate, how I may still not be as loving as I can be.

- I listen carefully to others' feedback rather than become defensive or ego aroused by it. I welcome feedback that shows me where I am less caring than I can be, where I am less tolerant, where less open. I am not afraid of free speech, my own or that of others. I am willing to express and to receive feelings, including fear, joy, grief, and tenderness. I show anger nonviolently, not in abusive, threatening, blaming, or out-of-control ways.

- I notice that my behavior and choices are no longer determined by what others may think of me. I am making no attempts to get others to accept or love me. I am not changing myself to fit in. I am committed to portraying myself just as I am, no matter what the reaction. I can no longer be manipulated by flattery, but I do show my thanks when others appreciate me.

- No matter what happens to me, I remain ever more grounded, unswayed by fear or desire. The events in life and the actions of others impact me, but they do not impinge. I remain secure within myself and, at the same time, connected to others.

- I forgo taking advantage of others by using any charms of body, word, or mind to trick or seduce them. To grow in humility, I blow the whistle on myself when I notice myself being phony, mendacious, passive-aggressive, or manipulative. I come clean right then and there by admitting that I am acting falsely. This is how I open myself to finding virtuous alternatives.

- I ask for what I want without demand, manipulation, or expectation. I remain respectful of the timing, wishes, and limits of others. I can take no for an answer.

• I am less and less competitive in relationships and find an up-lifting joy in cooperation. I especially shun situations in which my winning means that others have to lose.

• I do not knowingly hurt others. If they hurt me, I do not retali-ate, only open a dialogue and ask for amends. No matter what, I do not hate anyone or hold grudges. I act kindly toward others not to im-press or obligate them but because I really am kind—or working on it. If others fail to thank me or to return my kindness, that does not stop me from being loving nonetheless. I never give up on others. I be-lieve that everyone has an innate goodness and that being loved can release it. I am committed to resisting evil and fighting injustice in nonviolent ways. This is how I focus on restorative justice, not ret-ributive justice.

• I have a sense of humor but not at the expense of others. I do not engage in ridicule or sarcasm, or do I use "comebacks" when others are sarcastic toward me. I simply feel the pain in both of us and look for ways to bring more effectiveness into our communication.

• I look at other people and their choices without censure. I still notice the shortcomings of others and of myself, but I see them as facts rather than flaws. I do not laugh at people's mistakes or misfortunes.

• I am able to say "Ouch!" to pain and abuse in jobs, relationships, and interactions with others. I take action to change what can be changed and to move on when things remain abusive. I do this with-out self-pity or the need to make others wrong.

• I abide by standards of rigorous honesty and truthfulness in all my dealings no matter how others act toward me. My question is not "What can I get away with?" but "What is the right thing to do?" If I fall down in this, I admit it, make amends, and resolve to act differ-ently next time. I easily and willingly apologize when necessary.

• I am focusing on being consistent: At home or in relationship I am the same person I am at work. I show the same respect and sin-cerity toward strangers as I show toward those close to me.

• I keep my word. I honor commitments and I follow through on the tasks I agree to do. More and more I can tell what my limits and skills are. This helps me set sane boundaries on how much I offer to do for others, rather than simply being accommodating.

- I have an unwavering sense of myself as a person of conviction while still remaining flexible. I am able to change my behavior, to drop outmoded beliefs, and to make alterations in my lifestyle to fit the ever-evolving demands of my world. When I come up against an identity crisis, I take it as an opportunity for enlightenment.

- I am thankful for the values and helpful beliefs that I received in the course of my life from so many sources. At the same time, I am examining the scaffoldings of beliefs, biases, and myths I inherited from family, school, religion, and society. One by one, I dismantle and discard those not in keeping with healthy and virtuous living and cherish those that are.

- I am no longer under the blinding influence of the four main streets that direct so many attitudes and lifestyles: Madison Avenue, Tin Pan Alley, Wall Street, and Hollywood Boulevard.

- I measure my success by how much steadfast love I have, not by how much I have in the bank nor by how much power I have over others. Expressing my full and unique capacity to love is the central focus of my life.

- I am engaged enthusiastically in meaningful work and projects, and that is the source of my bliss. I keep discovering my deepest needs, wishes, values, and potentials and living in accord with them. I have reason to be proud of some accomplishments. Thoreau wrote in his journal: "A man looks with pride at his woodpile." My serious commitment to the practices on these pages is my "woodpile."

- I ask this question as I embark upon any project or relationship: Is this a suitable context for me to fulfill my life purpose? My life purpose is to live the unique and exuberant life that is inside me, to love with all my might, and to share my personal gifts in any way and everywhere I can.

- I am willing to work indefatigably to fulfill my life purpose but not to stress my health to acquire standing, status, fame, or fortune, the central and often only values in the ego's worried world. My focus in life is simply on becoming a good person.

- My work on myself has made me more conscious of the politics and stresses of the world around me. I question authority while affirming, praying, and working for an end to war, retaliation, greed, hate, and ignorance. This is based on the fact that I have not given up on believing in the possibility of transformation for every person, political and religious leader, and nation.

• I am always aware of the pain and poverty of those less fortunate than I. I find ways to respond that combine generosity and personal contact. I am generous with time, attention, money, and myself.

• Confronted with the suffering in the world, I do not turn my eyes away, nor do I get stuck in blaming God or humanity but simply ask: "What then shall *I* do?" I respond to pain in others with a plan to help, even if it has to be minimal. I choose to light one candle rather than curse the darkness. The poet T. S. Eliot wrote: "I sat upon the shore / . . . with the arid plain behind me. / Shall I at least set *my* lands in order?" (my italics) (The self-question and the quotation in this paragraph show how personal commitment to virtue helps us live *with* reality rather than in opposition to it. Spiritual practice makes the most distressing givens of our world bearable.)

• My love of nature makes me tread gently on the earth with what Saint Bonaventura called "a courtesy toward natural things."

• I can feel myself growing in spiritual consciousness. I can feel a divine energy within me that is behind whatever love, wisdom, or healing power I may have or show. What is in me is not from me but through me. I say thanks for these encouraging graces and yes to the stirring call to keep living up to them.

As I say yes to the givens of life, may I live in serene equanimity through storm and calm, clarity and uncertainty, gain and loss, praise and blame, and may I become a fulcrum of balance in ego's unwieldy world.

EPILOGUE

The Givens That Are Our Graces

*Sometimes it happens that we receive the power to say yes
to ourselves, that peace enters into us whole, that self-hate
and self-contempt disappear, and that our self is reunited
with itself. Then we can say that grace has come upon us.*
— Paul Tillich

In this book I have named and explored five givens of life and
relationships that we too often deny and ignore, causing ourselves
pain and unhappiness. These are the "negative" truths that we often
wish weren't so, but I have demonstrated how our resistance to these
facts of life is really where our troubles lie. When we open to the
givens, we open to the possibility of becoming the courageous, compassionate, and wise beings we were meant to be.

But it's important to remember that we humans also come
equipped with beautiful, positive givens. They are our gifts, graces
that are part of our collective human inheritance and come from
powers beyond ego. And they are graces in the dancer's sense too,
charming, elegant refinements of how we move in the world. These
graces are what make us truly human:

Our irrepressible playfulness and sense of humor
Our ability to go on loving no matter how we are treated by others
    and no matter what happened to us in the past
Our outrage at and courageous action in the face of evil

Our willingness to put ourselves second, even to risk our life for
    others
Our capacity to forgive and let go
Our refusal to accept defeat or abuse in the face of any odds
Our unflappable hope
Our knack for showing our best when things are at their worst
Our skill at finding order in chaos and meaning in disaster
Our intuition, which reveals more than we logically know
Our tendency to be honest even when no one is looking
Our striving for what lies beyond our grasp, our inclination to stretch
    ourselves
Our power to say, do, or be something that leads to healing ourselves
    and others
Our abiding sense that the universe is friendly and that there is ulti-
    mately a loving intent in all that happens
Our kindly understanding of and loving reaching out to those who do
    not choose to live in accord with this list

These graces are why we never give up on ourselves or others.
There will always be enough time for any of us to be touched and con-
verted by grace so that the givens may bloom: We can always change,
find our destined plan, act fairly and even generously, live through
pain, and show unconditional love.

We open ourselves to such graces when we feel a sense of accompaniment by a protecting presence that abides even when we want to
give up on ourselves. This sense does not have to be a matter of superstition or wishful thinking. Ultimately the universe is a holding
environment, and holding feels personal, so it is natural to sense a
kindly, personally loving presence in our lives. Such a sense, held in
human consciousness so long, is the equivalent of a reality. What are
some of the signs, however subjective, of the spiritual given of a reliable presence—the archetype of the assisting force in the heroic
journey?

• We retain and enjoy a felt sense of accompaniment, of not being
alone as we face things in life. This arises in those special moments of

synchronicity and grace that make us realize that our ego is not all that we have going for us.

• There are resources in and around us and they appear at any time but particularly in our moments of unconditional yes, trust, meditation, prayer, imagination, vision, or intuition.

• We experience moments in which we feel that we are in contact with the source of love, wisdom, and healing—indeed, that we are that.

• We notice an abiding sense of someone or something that earnestly wants us to evolve and to fulfill our potential. This comforting presence is on our side, rooting for us, focused on us without condition, judgment, restraint, pause, or stint.

• We notice we are being given graces that help us realize our wholeness. They take many forms: the givens themselves, particular people, places, things, dreams, or synchronous events that point out our path and help us traverse it. People in our lives who help or hurt us seem particularly to be messengers, mostly unwittingly, from just such a higher source.

• We are sometimes in touch with spacious depths in ourselves and aware that those depths are the same as those in other beings and in all the universe. As long as nature is around us, we are enfolded in divine life, the life beyond conditions.

• We experience in nature and in our own psychic life a sense of wonder, awe, rich pathos; we reach sublime peaks of feeling; we encounter powers beyond human making that seem to reach out to us and never let us go. We feel mysteriously supported at times, and that support is what is meant by divine presence.

• We feel a sense of belonging, as if the natural world were holding us in a lifelong caress, like what we felt in our mother's arms and maybe now in our lover's arms.

• No matter how dark or destructive things become, we are aware of a healing energy ever afoot that indefatigably renews and rebuilds what falls apart. Something keeps putting it—and us—all back together. This is why it is all right to fall apart. The psalmist sings: "Yes, though I walk through the valley of the shadow of death, I will fear no evil." We fear no evil because we are willing to walk all the way down and through the scary valley rather than across a bridge above it.

• We palpably feel a loving purpose built into the very structure and direction of the universe. Why things happen is ultimately a mystery. We cannot exactly say that everything happens for a purpose. However, making the best of what happens to us is the equivalent of a purpose. The opportunity that comes from a painful event is, in effect, its purpose, its evolutionary direction. And the direction of evolution is always onward: "Our God is *marching on.*"

• We may feel personally loved when we look at religious images and when we appreciate nature. We feel there is a power in the universe, and at the same time beyond it, that loves us as we uniquely are, accepts us, attends to us, hears us, values us, and that at the same time allows us to reject it and yet never gives up on us.

• We have it in us to go on loving in trying circumstances and with trying people, and this makes us feel confident that love is our origin, purpose, and end. How sanguine and yet inscrutable that our human energies can mediate such miraculous powers!

• We sense that the world and we are one single mysterious energy, at once transitory and everlasting, at once given and gift. "I am what nature is" becomes an answer to the conditions of existence. It is the answer of belonging.

• This loving presence is not necessarily experienced as personal, as in the traditional religious belief. Our capacity to hold the sense of a presence can be the equivalent of what is meant by the presence of God. For instance, our capacity to go on loving, no matter how harshly we have been treated, is the metaphorical equivalent of trusting that "God draws good out of evil."

• Our deepest inner life has recognized itself as God or saints or Buddha, none of which are separate persons but archetypal personifications of an ineffable, infallible, and inextinguishable light in us and in all that is. God, or buddha nature, is a personification of the essential being that keeps finding itself through the conscious evolution of each of us.

• A belief survives in us that there is something, we know not what, that is always lovingly at work, we know not how, to make the world more than it is now, to make us more than we are yet. That something is our own lively energy and simultaneously the life force of the universe.

It is a gift that we are star stuff, and so built into us is an undying urge toward the evolutionary transformation that is variously called wholeness, sanctity, enlightenment. We are not alone in this; all creation joins us. We can hear the longing of the entire universe. It is audible now in the unique groan for completeness that is arising from every one of us. That completeness comes to life whenever our love is aroused and bestowed. So, now we see, loving-kindness *is* human completeness.

As I say yes to the givens of life, may I live in continual awareness of being held with love by a caring presence that never deserts me, and may I hold others in such a way that they begin to trust that presence too.

ABOUT THE AUTHOR

Dᴀᴠɪᴅ Rɪᴄʜᴏ, Ph.D., M.F.T., is a psychotherapist, teacher, and writer who emphasizes Jungian, transpersonal, and spiritual perspectives in his work. He teaches at Santa Barbara City College, Adult Education; University of California at Berkeley Extension; and Esalen.

He is the author of:

How to Be an Adult: A Handbook on Psychological and Spiritual Integration (Paulist Press, 1991)

When Love Meets Fear: How to Become Defense-Less and Resource-Full (Paulist Press, 1997)

Unexpected Miracles: The Gift of Synchronicity and How to Open It (Crossroad, 1998)

Shadow Dance: Liberating the Power and Creativity of Your Dark Side (Shambhala Publications, 1999)

Catholic Means Universal: Integrating Spirituality and Religion (Crossroad, 2000)

Mary Within: A Jungian Contemplation of Her Titles and Powers (Crossroad, 2001)

How to Be an Adult in Relationships: The Five Keys to Mindful Loving (Shambhala Publications, 2002)

David Richo gives workshops across the country, some of which are available on audiotape. For a catalog, send a self-addressed legal-size envelope with a single stamp to David Richo, Box 31027, Santa Barbara, CA 93130.

Visit *davericho.com* for a complete listing of workshops, books, and audiotapes.